HEROES, JEDIS, & DUDES
The Brand Archetype Field Guide for Founders, Marketers, and Other Rebels

By Paul Molinari

Heroes, Jedis, and Dudes
The Brand Archetype Field Guide for Founders, Marketers, and Other Rebels

Popcorn Marketing Group, LLC
info@popcorngtm.com
popcorngtm.com

Disclaimer: The information in this book is provided for general educational and informational purposes only. While the author and publisher have made every effort to ensure the accuracy of the content, they make no warranties or representations as to its completeness or applicability to any particular business, brand, or situation. The frameworks, strategies, and examples shared in this book are based on the author's professional experience and are not a substitute for tailored marketing, legal, or business advice. The author and publisher assume no liability for any loss or damage arising from the use of the information contained herein. Results will vary. Brands mentioned are the property of their respective owners and are referenced for illustrative and commentary purposes only.

Trademarks: Popcorn GTM™, Popcorn Brand Deck™, Air Cover™ and related marks are trademarks of Popcorn Marketing Group, LLC. All other trademarks, service marks, and trade names referenced in this book are the property of their respective owners.

Cover and interior design by Paul Molinari
Printed in the United States of America
ISBN: 9798258384942

Contents

Heroes, Jedis, and Dudes

AUTHOR'S NOTE:
Why This Book Exists

Whenever I tell someone that my company is called Popcorn, they smile.

That feels pretty good. It also tells me something immediately about the person. Whether they are curious about the why, or whether they just move on. The curious ones are usually my people.

Here is the why.

About ten years ago, I stumbled across a Web 1.0 blog by a former McKinsey consultant named David Klein. His blog was called The Popped Kernel. I don't remember how I found it. I don't remember what else was on it. But I remember one idea, and it lodged in my brain and stayed there for a decade.

The idea was this: we are all kernels. Some of us have popped. Others have not. Yet.

Klein wrote about what a kernel actually needs to pop. The conditions have to be right. The kernel can't be too hard. The heat has to be right — too little and nothing happens, too much and it burns. Once popped, it needs to cool before it's any good to anyone. Leave it idle too long and it goes stale. The kernel is fragile. The conditions matter enormously.

I kept thinking about that image whenever I felt stuck. Is there anything worse than an unpopped kernel? Sitting at the bottom of the bucket. Hard. Burnt. Small. A promise that didn't happen.

When I started this company, I knew the name immediately.

Popcorn. Because the whole point is helping brands pop. Giving them the right conditions: the heat, the pressure, the creative energy to become what they were supposed to be all along. Not holding anything back. Not settling for the bottom of the bucket.

But here is the thing I didn't fully understand when I named the company.

I thought what brands needed to pop was better marketing. Better execution. The right tactics, the right channels, the right campaign structure.

I was right about some of that. I was missing the most important part.

I spent close to a decade helping scale a restaurant technology company from an emerging player into a category leader. I watched great products fail to connect. I watched companies with genuine solutions produce messaging that sounded exactly like every other company in the space. I watched founders who knew exactly why their thing mattered produce websites that said nothing about it.

The problem was never the product. The problem was almost never the execution.

The problem was that nobody knew who the brand was.

Not in the way that matters. Not at the bone. Not the archetype-level identity that shapes everything: the voice, the story, the audience you attract, the position you own in someone's mind. That layer was missing. And without it, all the marketing in the world is just expensive noise produced quickly.

No textbook I read in undergrad or grad school ever mentioned this. I went looking. The frameworks were there. The five-step processes were there. The Buyer's Black Box and the Marketing Concept and the segmentation matrices. All of it is technically complete.

None of it mentioned soul.

None of it explained why some brands make people feel something and other brands, with nearly identical products and perfectly executed campaigns, produce nothing but indifference.

This book is my answer to that absence.

It is built from years of working inside brands that were stuck. From watching the moment a founder finally understands who their brand actually is and seeing the clarity that follows. From the Popcorn GTM work of helping restaurant tech companies, foodservice innovators, and growth-stage founders find the identity that was always there — just unnamed, unexpressed, and unaligned with everything they were putting into the market.

It is also built from the Brand Deck, which started as a workshop tool and became a 53-card system for exactly this work. The archetypes. The story frameworks. The voice tools. The audience insights. The activation prompts. Cards that force the right questions and produce real answers.

I am a Rebel and an Explorer, if you want to know my archetype. I distrust the default. I get bored by the safe answer. I find the conventional marketing playbook aesthetically offensive: the jargon, the hedging, the copy that could belong to anyone because it was written to offend no one.

That energy is in every page of this book. I hope it serves you.

You know the metaphor by now.

The kernel needs the right conditions to pop. It cannot be too hard. The heat has to be right. Idle too long, it goes stale.

Your brand is the kernel.

The archetype is the heat.

This book is your conditions.

Go make it pop.

Paul Molinari

Founder & Principal, Popcorn Marketing Group, LLC
Host, Modern Solutions for Modern Restaurants Podcast
www.popcorngtm.com

A little bit about the Author:

Hi, I'm Paul. I'm a marketing strategist, messaging expert, creative director, and maybe your next hire. This has been a long time coming. I started Popcorn, a fractional CMO agency, after nearly nine years leading marketing at Crunchtime, where I helped turn a scrappy restaurant tech company into the go-to brand for back-of-house software, working with names like Jersey Mike's Subs and AMC Theatres. Fittingly, Crunchtime became Popcorn's first client, and that kicked off this whole go-to-market agency journey.

Over the past two decades, I've shaped marketing strategies for brands big and small, at Digitas for clients like General Motors and AstraZeneca to tech players like Tweeter, Immuta, and Thomson. What's made it interesting is not just the variety -- data security, restaurants, cars, consumer A/V, healthcare, but the results: launching GM's Owner Center for millions of Cadillac and Chevy drivers, integrating a digital Rx sample closet on WebMD for Crestor, or helping catch the attention of investment powerhouse, Battery Ventures.

Receipts? I've led campaigns that have driven over $100 million in attributed revenue.

A trained graphic designer with an MBA - part creative, part data nerd - I bring that mix to everything I do. I studied marketing at Marist College and earned my MBA from Northeastern's D'Amore-McKim School of Business.

These days, I'm based on Boston's South Shore with my wife, three Gen-Z kids, and two dogs - Maverick and Rooster (we lost Goose). If you're ever in town, let's grab a Dunkin' or a Sam Adams -- first round's on me.

P.S.

When you create a "business book" outline, you take a lot of time considering how the bigger pieces of the story or instructions fit together. When thinking about the structure of this book, I knew that I wanted to dig deep into a few areas.

First, the archetypes – really getting into them from a storytelling perspective shaped around marketing fundamentals and brand psychology. I also knew I wanted to question traditional marketing textbooks, because I don't believe many take the Power of Brand seriously - which to me, is remarkable. Then, a remarkable thing happened. I landed inside the real meatballs and parmesan of this whole book

- the Popcorn Brand Deck system creation. I love playing cards, baseball cards, note cards, D&D, credit cards... anything that's got a cool design on one side and a little story on the other that lets you use your imagination. Anyhow, I think it's really something special and I will publish a "card" system soon with all the story frameworks and archetypes in a properly packaged "card deck.". In the meantime... it's all in the book.

So, thanks for letting me dump my wild and disparate data into your crystal clear lake, friend. There's fresh fish in those newly muddied waters.

Now, let's enjoy the fire.

- PM

INTRODUCTION:
Why Most Brands Are Invisible

Here is the official definition of marketing, as approved by the American Marketing Association, the professional body that has governed this discipline since 1937:

"The activity, set of institutions, and processes for creating, communicating, delivering, and exchanging offerings that have value for customers, clients, partners, and society at large."

Twenty-six words. Not a single one of them is "meaning." Not one is "identity." Not one is "story."

This is not a small omission. This is the whole problem.

Let me tell you about the invisible brands.

They are everywhere. You've seen them at trade shows. You've scrolled past them on LinkedIn. You've sat in pitch meetings while someone walked through their slide deck, a deck that looked polished and checked every box and said absolutely nothing.

Good product. Solid team. Reasonable price. Clear value proposition. And nobody cares.

Not because the product is bad. The product might be genuinely great. Not because the team lacks talent. Not because the market doesn't exist. Invisible brands fail because they never answered the only question that actually matters before any of the other questions:

Who are you?

Not what do you do. Not who is your target customer. Not what is your competitive advantage. Who ARE you, at the level of identity, instinct, and meaning? What is the role your brand was born to play? What archetype lives at the center of everything you make, say, and stand for?

Most brands skip this question entirely. They jump straight to the 4Ps. Product, Price, Place, Promotion. They build personas and do research and create messaging matrices and run A/B tests and then wonder why nothing resonates.

The house is built. The plumbing works. Nobody wants to live there.

Here is what I have noticed after years of working inside brands, building brands, and helping founders figure out why their very good products were not connecting with very real audiences:

The brands that break through are not always the best products. They are not always the best-funded. They are not always the most technically sophisticated or the first to market.

The brands that break through are the ones that mean something.

Not something vague and corporate. Not "we are committed to excellence in service delivery." Something real. Something you can feel. Something that makes a certain kind of person see their brand and think, immediately and viscerally: that's mine.

Harley-Davidson does not make the best motorcycle on the market by any objective measure. They make the soul of the American Rebel. And people will pay three times the price and wait six months on a list and tattoo the logo on their arm, for that.

Nike does not make the only athletic shoe. There are better-engineered shoes, more comfortable shoes, cheaper shoes. Nike sells the belief that you have something in you worth fighting for. That is The Hero speaking. And The Hero has been speaking through every ad, every product launch, and every "Just Do It" for decades without losing its voice.

Apple does not make computers. Apple makes the feeling that the people who use them are different. Creatives. Visionaries. People who see the world not as it is but as it could be. That is The Magician at work. And when Steve Jobs said "one more thing," the world stopped.

What do these brands have in common? They know who they are. They claimed an archetype, whether they used that word for it or not, and they built everything around it. The product, the price, the messaging, the design, the way they hire, the way they fire, the way they show up at 9am on a Tuesday and at midnight during a crisis. All of it consistent. All of it recognizable. All of it pointing back to the same core identity.

That is not an accident. That is architecture.

Carl Jung called them archetypes. A Swiss psychologist writing in the early 20th century, Jung observed something that has held up across a century of research: certain characters, certain roles, certain patterns of behavior appear in every culture on earth, across every era of human history.

The Hero who faces impossible odds. The Rebel who defies the order. The Sage who speaks truth. The Explorer who ventures beyond the map. The Caregiver who shows up. The Jester who tells the truth by making you laugh.

These are not invented. They are inherited. They live in the part of the brain that predates language and logic, the part that responds before you can stop it. When you see Indiana Jones step into the torchlit temple and smirk, something fires in you that you did not choose. When you watch the underdog run through the rain and reach the summit, something rises in your chest. When someone in power finally gets their comeuppance, you feel a satisfaction older than justice.

Joseph Campbell spent his career mapping these patterns across mythology, literature, and religion. He found the same stories told in ancient Mesopotamia, medieval Europe, feudal Japan, and modern Hollywood. The specifics change. The deep structure never does.

Brands tap into this. The best ones always have. The question is whether they do it consciously or by accident. This book is about doing it on purpose.

There are 12 archetypes. You will meet all of them in this book.

The Hero, The Rebel, The Explorer, The Sage, The Magician, The Caregiver, The Creator, The Jester, The Lover, The Ruler, The Innocent, The Everyperson. Each one has a distinct identity, a distinct voice, a distinct relationship with its audience, and a distinct place in the culture. Each one attracts a specific kind of person for a specific kind of reason.

Your brand is one of them. Possibly two, with one as dominant. But not six. Not all twelve. Trying to be all twelve is the brand equivalent of trying to be everyone's best friend. You end up with a personality no one can describe and an audience that doesn't know why they should care.

When you find your archetype, something shifts. The messaging questions get easier. The voice questions get easier. Hiring gets easier. Content gets easier. You stop trying to say something clever and start saying something true. The truth of who you are, told to the people who need exactly that.

Here is what this book covers, and here is what it is for.

Part One is the archetypes themselves. Not just a definition. A full portrait of each one: the character, the voice, the visual world, the right conditions to claim it, the brands that live there, and the honest red flags when it's being used badly. You will find your archetype here. Not by taking a quiz that spits out a result. By reading and recognizing. By the moment of yes that happens when you see the description of the one that fits.

Part Two is storytelling. Once you know who you are, you need to know how to tell your story. There are 12 frameworks in this book, not formulas, scaffolding. Structure that lets your truth breathe. The Hero's Journey, the Pixar Pitch, the Villain-Solution-Victory. The right framework for your archetype, your audience, your moment.

Part Three is voice. This is where it gets personal and specific. Voice is not your tagline. Voice is the fingerprint of your brand on every word you write, every piece of content you publish, every conversation your team has with a customer. Voice is what makes someone read a paragraph and think: that sounds like them. This section gives you the tools to build that fingerprint deliberately and protect it over time.

Part Four is your audience. Because even the sharpest archetype and the clearest voice lands nowhere if you are aiming at the wrong people, or worse, aiming at everyone. The right audience for a Hero brand is not the same as the right audience for a Caregiver brand. Understanding the difference, and knowing how to find the people who are already inclined to believe in you, changes everything.

Part Five is activation. Which is just a word for: do something with all of this. Build the playbook. Ship the content. Make the brand real in the world. Because the most beautifully defined archetype that never shows up anywhere is a strategy document sitting in a folder. This section is about making sure that doesn't happen.

This book is not a textbook. You may have read textbooks. You may have paid a lot of money for textbooks. I have nothing against textbooks - and the pictures are usually cool. They do what they say they do: they teach you the mechanics of the discipline.

But here is what the mechanics do not teach you: why some brands feel like a cold room and others feel like a fire.

Mechanics are the plumbing. Archetypes are what flows through it.

If you have been doing the work, applying the frameworks, optimizing the campaigns, checking every box, and still wondering why it is not connecting the way you hoped, this book is the missing piece. Not because the frameworks were wrong. Because the foundation under the frameworks was never laid.

That foundation is identity. That identity is your archetype.

One last thing before we begin.

Marketing textbooks love formulas. One of the most famous is the Value Equation. Customer value, the textbook tells you, is the ratio of perceived benefits to price. The formula looks like this:

$$V = B \ / \ P$$

Value equals Benefits divided by Price. Tidy, logical, and completely insufficient for explaining why people cry at Apple product launches.

Or why Supreme customers camp overnight for a hoodie.

Or why someone would rather ride a Harley in a rainstorm than drive a Honda Civic in comfort.

Or why a restaurant that charges four times the market rate for a bowl of ramen has a two-hour wait every night.

The formula is real. It works. At the level of commodity, it explains a lot of purchasing behavior. But there is a category of brand relationship that the formula cannot touch. The brands that become tribal. The brands that become part of who their customers believe themselves to be. The brands where "I use this" is a statement about identity, not just preference.

That gap between the formula and the feeling is where this book lives.

The textbook gave you the equation. This book gives you the thing that makes the equation irrelevant.

Let's go find your archetype.

"The myth is the public dream. The dream is the private myth."

-- Joseph Campbell

How to use this book: Read it straight through once if you are starting fresh. Use it as a field guide after that. Return to the chapter that covers your archetype whenever you are writing something that matters. Keep the Brand Deck nearby. The 53 cards are the portable version of everything in here.

The Brand Deck companion cards are referenced throughout each chapter. They are the workshop version of this book: exercises, prompts, and tools you can use alone or with a team to translate insight into action.

Next: Part One. The Myth Beneath Your Message.

Chapter 1: What the Hell Is a Brand Archetype?

CHAPTER 1:
What the Hell Is a Brand Archetype?

"The cave you fear to enter holds the treasure you seek."

-- Joseph Campbell

THE TEXTBOOK VERSION

Consumer buying behavior works like a stimulus-response model. Marketing inputs go in. Environmental inputs go in. Then everything passes through something called the buyer's "black box," which is acknowledged as largely unknown and mysterious, like a locked room the textbook doesn't have a key to. Outputs come out: product choice, brand choice, purchase timing. Master the inputs, influence the outputs. The black box is just there, unnamed, unexplained, accepted as a given.

THE FIELD VERSION

The black box isn't empty.

It is packed full. Densely, specifically, magnificently full. Full of patterns so deeply wired into the human brain that they predate commerce, language, and the concept of a marketing budget by tens of thousands of years. Full of characters so universal that a child in Tokyo and a grandmother in Buenos Aires and a teenager in Lagos will each recognize them instantly without ever having met.

Carl Jung called them archetypes.

The textbook drew a diagram and moved on. This book opens the box.

The Man Who Named the Patterns

Carl Jung was a Swiss psychiatrist who spent his career trying to understand what lies beneath the surface of human thought. Not the conscious, rational, decision-making mind that fills out spreadsheets and compares prices. The other part. The older part. The part that dreams.

What Jung found, after decades of research and clinical work, was that certain images, figures, and patterns appeared with remarkable consistency across his patients, regardless of their backgrounds. He found the same patterns in the myths of ancient Greece, in Native American folklore, in Hindu sacred texts, and in the fairy tales of medieval Europe. Same characters. Same story shapes. Same emotional triggers. Different costumes, same cast.

He called these the archetypes of the collective unconscious. The idea was this: beneath the individual unconscious, which is personal and biographical, there exists a deeper layer shared by all of humanity. A kind of inherited library of characters and story patterns that every human being carries regardless of where or when they were born.

The Hero who rises to meet a challenge. The Sage who holds the wisdom that will save the day. The Rebel who refuses to be contained by the rules of the world. The Caregiver who sacrifices for those in their charge. The Explorer who pushes into unmapped territory. The Innocent who holds on to hope when the world has given up.

These are not invented. They are inherited. They are in you. They are in your customers. And when a brand taps into one of them, something happens that no amount of competitive pricing or feature optimization can replicate.

People feel it.

The Man Who Proved They're Universal

Joseph Campbell was an American professor of literature who spent his life doing something the academy considered slightly embarrassing: he took mythology seriously.

Not as historical curiosity. Not as anthropological data. As living truth.

Campbell's most important contribution is what he called the monomyth, also known as the Hero's Journey. After studying the myths, legends, and sacred stories of hundreds of cultures across thousands of years, Campbell identified a single underlying story structure that appeared in all of them.

A hero lives in an ordinary world. A call comes, an adventure beckons, a challenge arrives that the hero cannot ignore. The hero resists at first (this is human). Then crosses the threshold into an unfamiliar world. Faces trials, enemies, temptations, and the darkest possible moment. Finds within themselves what they need. Wins, transforms, and returns home changed, carrying something of value for the people they left behind.

You have seen this story ten thousand times. Star Wars. The Odyssey. Harry Potter. The Lion King. Rocky. The Matrix. Moana. Every superhero origin story ever told. The specifics are always different. The structure is always the same.

Why? Campbell's answer: because this is the shape of human transformation. It is not a literary device. It is a map of how people actually change. And because we all know this journey in our bones, we recognize it instantly when we see it, and we feel it when we don't.

This matters to your brand in a direct and urgent way. Your customer has a Hero's Journey. They have a challenge they are trying to overcome, a transformation they are trying to make, a version of themselves they are trying to reach. The brands that last are the ones that find their place in that journey. Not as the hero. As the guide. As the Sage who hands the sword. As the Explorer who drew the map. As the Magician who shows what is possible.

More on that in Part Two.

For now, the point is this: Campbell proved that the patterns Jung named are not European. Not Western. Not modern. They are human. Every person on earth walks around carrying the same emotional software, loaded at birth, updated by culture, but never fundamentally replaced.

Your brand can speak to that software. Or it can keep sending press releases.

Heroes, Jedis, and Dudes

Here is a simple test.

I am going to name three characters. As I name each one, notice what happens in your body. Not what you think. What you feel.

Rocky Balboa.

Got it? Whatever just happened in you, the slight lift in the chest, the faint urge to clench your fist, the distant sound of trumpets climbing a flight of museum steps, that is The Hero archetype firing. Rocky is the club fighter from South Philly who had no business being in the ring with the heavyweight champion of the world. He went anyway. He didn't win the first fight. He didn't have to. He went the distance, and that was the point. The Hero doesn't know if they can win. They show up. That resonates with something real in people, because most people are trying to do exactly that in some part of their life.

Yoda.

Different response, right? Slower. Quieter. Heavier in a good way. Yoda is The Sage. Ancient. Patient. Sees things others cannot see. Does not chase the fight, holds the knowledge. When Yoda speaks, the universe seems slightly more organized. There is comfort in that. There is authority that has nothing to do with rank or title and everything to do with earned understanding. The Sage doesn't tell you what to do. The Sage shows you what is true. That is a completely different relationship, and you felt the difference before you could explain it.

The Dude.

The Big Lebowski. White Russian in hand. Bathrobe. Zero interest in your drama. Just wants to bowl, man. The Dude is The Everyperson. Unheroic by design. Not trying to save anyone. Not the wisest in the room. Just a guy, dealing with things, somehow maintaining an uncanny inner peace through the chaos of a world that makes no sense. The reason The Dude became a cultural icon with a genuine philosophical movement named after him is not because people want to be Jeff Bridges in a bathrobe. It is because The

Everyperson gives permission to be exactly who you are. No performance required. That hits something real too. Just differently.

Three archetypes. Three completely distinct emotional registers. Three kinds of people in the world who self-select toward them. And you felt the difference in your gut before your brain finished processing the names.

That is what archetypes do. They speak below the noise.

Now imagine building a brand around each one.

A Hero brand says: you have more in you than you know. Challenge accepted. Rise. Nike has said exactly this for forty years and never had to explain it.

A Sage brand says: let me show you what is actually true. We know, and we will tell you, clearly and without agenda. Google has said this since the first day someone typed a question into that white box and got a real answer.

An Everyperson brand says: no pretense. No performance. We are all just people here. IKEA has said this in every showroom, every flat-pack box, every meatball. They are not aspirational. They are recognized. There is a difference, and for certain audiences, recognition is more powerful than aspiration.

This is not a metaphor. This is the operating system.

What a Brand Archetype Actually Is

Let's be specific, because the word "archetype" gets tossed around in marketing circles the way "authentic" and "disruptive" do, loudly and without content.

A brand archetype is the core identity your brand embodies. Not the aesthetic. Not the tagline. Not the personality keywords in your brand guidelines. The fundamental character your brand plays in the relationship it has with its audience.

It answers the question: if your brand were a person, what kind of person would it be? Not what would they look like. What would they be about? What would they stand for? How would they walk into a room? What would they never do?

A brand archetype is not:

A mood board. Pretty pictures and color palettes and "we want to feel like a warm Saturday morning" are brand aesthetics. Useful, but not archetype.

A list of adjectives. "Bold, innovative, trustworthy, human-centered" is a brand strategy deck written by a committee. Any one of those adjectives could describe any of the 12 archetypes. Adjectives without an identity underneath them are decoration.

A target persona. Knowing that your customer is a 34-year-old operations manager who listens to podcasts on her commute tells you something about her. It tells you nothing about who you are to her. Archetype answers that.

A positioning statement. "We help mid-market SaaS companies reduce churn through data-driven customer success workflows" is a positioning statement. True, probably. Memorable? You tell me.

What a brand archetype IS:

The source code that makes all of the above consistent.

When you know your archetype, the adjectives become obvious. The aesthetic becomes obvious. The positioning statement gets a soul. The persona finds a reason to care about you. Everything that was a collection of separate decisions becomes a coherent identity.

It is not the roof of the house. It is the foundation. Everything else is built on it, or not built at all.

Why This Works at the Instinct Level

Here is the uncomfortable truth about the buying decisions your customers make.

Most of them are not rational.

This is not an insult to your customers. It is neuroscience. The brain makes emotional assessments before the rational mind has time to weigh in. By the time a person can consciously evaluate the features and pricing of two competing products, they have already formed a preference based on factors they are not aware of. Brand familiarity. Visual recognition. Emotional association. The feeling a company gives them when they encounter it.

The conscious mind then does what the conscious mind does: it constructs a rational explanation for the decision that was already made. "I chose this brand because of the quality." "I chose this because of the price-to-value ratio." "I chose this because of the reviews."

Maybe. Or maybe you chose it because it felt like you. Because it reflected back a version of yourself you want to believe in. Because something about it fired a pattern in your brain that you have been carrying since before you could read.

Archetypes operate at that level. Not at the level of features and benefits, though features and benefits matter. At the level of identity. At the level of meaning.

This is why Nike can charge more than the market for a running shoe and have people line up for the privilege.

This is why Harley-Davidson customers tattooed the logo on their bodies before loyalty programs were invented.

This is why Apple's product announcements generate the kind of emotional response usually reserved for religious experiences.

None of those brands won on specs. They won on archetype. They found their character, committed to it at every layer of the organization, and never let go.

The 12 Archetypes: A First Look

Jung identified a number of archetypes, and scholars have debated the full list ever since. For the purpose of brand strategy, 12 archetypes have emerged as the most consistently applicable, clear, and actionable. This is the system this book uses.

They are organized by the primary human motivation each one speaks to:

Freedom: The Rebel, The Explorer, The Magician. These archetypes appeal to the desire to break free, discover, and transform.

Social: The Hero, The Lover, The Jester. These archetypes operate through strength, connection, and play.

Order: The Caregiver, The Creator, The Ruler. These archetypes build, nurture, and control.

Belonging: The Everyperson, The Sage, The Innocent. These archetypes offer acceptance, wisdom, and comfort.

You will meet all 12 in the next chapter, with enough depth to orient yourself. Then in Chapter 3, you go deep. Each archetype gets its full portrait, its voice, its visual world, its red flags, and its activation challenges.

For now, here is the only thing you need to know:

One of these is yours.

Not two or three or a blend of seven. One primary archetype, possibly with a secondary influence that adds texture. But one dominant identity, consistently expressed, that your brand was built to inhabit.

And if you do not know which one it is yet, that is exactly what we are here to figure out.

Identity Versus Aesthetic: The Line Most Brands Miss

Before we move on, this distinction matters enough to make explicit.

Brand identity and brand aesthetic are not the same thing. They live in different layers, do different work, and most brands confuse them at significant cost.

Brand aesthetic is everything you can see. Your logo, your colors, your typography, your photography style, your social media grid, your packaging, your website layout. Aesthetic is presentation. It matters. It is often the first thing anyone notices about you. But it is not who you are. It is how you dress.

Brand identity is what persists when the aesthetic changes. It is the character underneath the clothes. Apple has redesigned its aesthetic multiple times in forty years. The identity, curious, elegant, slightly rebellious, visionary, has never changed. The Magician has been consistent throughout. That consistency is why decades of design evolution feel like the same company, not a series of rebrands.

When brands confuse aesthetic for identity, they redecorate instead of rebuild. New logo, new colors, new tagline, same forgettable character. They spend money changing how they look without touching who they are. The result is a brand that looks different and feels exactly the same.

The question this book is asking is the identity question. Who are you? Not how do you look.

When you have a real answer to the identity question, the aesthetic question becomes almost simple. You know what kind of world your brand inhabits. You know what kind of voice it speaks in. The visual decisions that used to feel arbitrary start to have a logic. The writing that used to sound like everyone else starts to sound like you.

One Thing Before We Meet the 12

A word about authenticity, because it is going to come up and it is going to matter.

Archetypes are not costumes. You do not pick the archetype that sounds coolest or the one that seems most on-trend for your category. You do not look at your competitor's archetype and choose a different one for differentiation purposes only. You do not pick the Rebel because Rebel brands seem to get attention, even though everything about your company is orderly, meticulous, and deeply committed to doing things the right way.

The archetype that works is the true one. The one that reflects something real about the founders, the culture, the reason the company was built. The one that, when you name it, people on the team say: yes, obviously, that's us.

This book is going to help you find that one.

There will be archetypes that feel appealing but wrong, like wearing someone else's jacket. There will be archetypes that feel obvious in a way that initially seems too simple, and those are usually the right ones. The best brand identities are not complicated. They are clear.

Clear is hard. Clear is what we are building toward.

Now let's meet the 12.

Brand Deck Connection: Summary Card 1, Brand Archetypes.

The card gives you the quick-reference version of everything in this chapter: the 12 archetypes organized by family, the core question each one answers, and the self-assessment prompt to start identifying your own. Pull it out now if you have it. Use this chapter and the next as the full context behind it.

Next: Chapter 2. The 12 Archetypes, A Field Guide.

CHAPTER 2:
The 12 Archetypes: A Field Guide

"Know thyself."

-- The Oracle at Delphi. Also good brand strategy.

This chapter is a first look, not a final answer.

You are going to meet all 12 archetypes here. Each one gets a portrait: who they are, how they sound, what they stand for, and which brands have claimed them. Read every single one, even the ones that feel immediately wrong for your brand. Especially those. Sometimes what you are not is as clarifying as what you are.

By the end of this chapter, you should have a strong instinct about where you belong. You will not have certainty yet. Certainty comes from Chapter 3, where each archetype gets its full treatment. But instinct is a good start. In fact, with archetypes, instinct is usually the most reliable compass you have.

One more thing before we begin.

The 12 archetypes are organized into four families, based on the primary human motivation each one speaks to. Freedom. Social. Order. Belonging. These families are not rigid boxes. They are a map. They tell you what drives each archetype at the deepest level, which tells you something about the kind of person who is drawn to it and the kind of relationship they want to have with a brand.

Pay attention to the family, not just the archetype. It will tell you something useful.

THE FREEDOM FAMILY

The Rebel. The Explorer. The Magician.

Freedom-family archetypes speak to the desire to break out, push past limits, and transform what is possible. Their audiences are people who feel constrained by the existing order and are looking for something that gives them permission, tools, or inspiration to transcend it. These brands tend to generate fierce loyalty because they tap into a deep, restless human drive: the need to be more, go further, and refuse the ordinary.

The Rebel

"Rules were made to be broken."

The Rebel doesn't just challenge the status quo. The Rebel believes the status quo is the problem. This archetype thrives on disruption, provocation, and liberation. Not chaos for its own sake, but rebellion in service of freedom. The Rebel brand says to its audience: the world has been telling you how to live, what to buy, who to be. We don't buy that. And neither should you.

The Rebel's voice is bold, blunt, and unapologetic. It does not hedge. It does not ask permission. It says things other brands are afraid to say, and it means them.

The risk is arrogance. The Rebel brand that mistakes transgression for authenticity starts to feel like performance. The best Rebel brands have actual conviction underneath the rebellion. They are not provocative for attention. They are provocative because they genuinely disagree with the way things are.

Brands that live here: Harley-Davidson, BrewDog, Diesel, Gibson, Liquid Death, The North Face black label.

The Explorer

"Go your own way."

The Explorer is driven by one thing: the need to discover. New territory, new ideas, new versions of the self. The Explorer brand gives its audience permission to venture off the map and the tools to survive when they get there. There is an inherent restlessness to this archetype. It is never satisfied with the known. It always wants to know what is around the next bend.

The Explorer's voice is curious, independent, and alive. It does not prescribe. It invites. It asks "what if" more than it states "this is how." It honors the journey as much as the destination.

The risk is lack of focus. The Explorer brand that is always searching can feel ungrounded, always pivoting, never arriving. The best Explorer brands have a point of view underneath the wandering. They explore toward something, not just away from the ordinary.

Brands that live here: Patagonia, REI, Jeep, Airbnb, National Geographic.

The Magician

"Turn insight into alchemy."

The Magician transforms. Where others see a problem, the Magician sees an opportunity to make something impossible become real. This is the archetype of vision, of turning complexity into clarity, of making the audience feel like they are witnessing something that shouldn't be possible but somehow is. The Magician brand makes promises that sound too good and then delivers.

The Magician's voice is visionary, evocative, and slightly mysterious. It speaks in possibility rather than specification. It does not explain how the trick works. It invites you into the experience.

The risk is overpromising. The Magician that cannot deliver on its vision becomes a fraud. The best Magician brands have real substance behind the wonder: technology that actually works, results that actually materialize, transformation that actually happens.

Brands that live here: Apple, Disney, Tesla, Dyson, LUSH.

THE SOCIAL FAMILY

The Hero. The Lover. The Jester.

Social-family archetypes operate through human connection. The Hero connects through shared challenge and the will to overcome. The Lover connects through intimacy and desire. The Jester connects through laughter and shared irreverence. What unites them is the relationship: these brands are not talking at their audience. They are in it with them. The Social family produces the brands people most often describe as "feeling human."

The Hero

"Challenge accepted."

The Hero faces what others run from. Not because the Hero is fearless, but because the mission matters more than the fear. The Hero archetype speaks to the part of every person that wants to be capable, proven, and worthy of the challenge in front of them. The Hero brand says: you have more in you than you know. We are here to help you find it.

The Hero's voice is direct, motivated, and clear-eyed. It does not coddle. It believes in the audience enough to push them. It uses action verbs. It is more interested in what you will do than in how you feel.

The risk is exhaustion. The Hero brand that never lets up, that turns every communication into a call to battle, starts to feel relentless. The best Hero brands know when to acknowledge the struggle before calling for the next push.

Brands that live here: Nike, Under Armour, Peloton, the U.S. Army, Gatorade.

The Lover

"Feel something."

The Lover is about desire. Not just romantic desire, though that is part of it. The desire for beauty, for pleasure, for deep connection, for the experience of being fully present in a sensory moment. The Lover brand elevates the ordinary into something worth savoring. It makes its audience feel seen, chosen, and worthy of something extraordinary.

The Lover's voice is warm, intimate, and rich with sensory language. It speaks in texture and feeling. It does not rush. It lingers. It understands that the most powerful thing a brand can do is make someone feel genuinely desired.

The risk is superficiality. The Lover brand that is all surface and no substance mistakes aesthetics for identity. The best Lover brands have genuine quality underneath the beauty. The feeling is earned.

Brands that live here: Chanel, Häagen-Dazs, Godiva, Victoria's Secret, Bose.

The Jester

"Serious brands are seriously boring."

The Jester knows something the other archetypes sometimes forget: laughter is one of the most powerful forces in human connection. The Jester disarms, delights, and tells the truth in the one way that makes people lean in rather than defend: by making them laugh. The Jester brand is not afraid to look ridiculous. It is afraid of being forgettable.

The Jester's voice is playful, quick, and often genuinely weird. It surprises. It subverts. It would rather make you snort coffee out of your nose than nod respectfully at a well-crafted sentence.

The risk is being written off. The Jester brand that can only be funny struggles to be trusted with real decisions or serious money. The best Jester brands use humor as the vehicle, not the destination. The actual product or service is excellent. The wit just makes you want to find out.

Brands that live here: Old Spice, Liquid Death, Aviation Gin, Dollar Shave Club, early Duolingo.

THE ORDER FAMILY

The Caregiver. The Creator. The Ruler.

Order-family archetypes build, protect, and maintain. They give the world structure, nurture, and excellence. Their audiences are people who want stability, quality, and the comfort of knowing that someone with taste and authority is in charge. These brands generate trust through consistency. They are the ones you come back to. They are the ones that feel like they will still be here in twenty years.

The Caregiver

"We've got you."

The Caregiver exists to protect and serve. Not from obligation, but from genuine concern for the people in its care. The Caregiver brand prioritizes the audience's wellbeing above its own agenda. It shows up when things get hard, speaks gently when others speak loudly, and earns loyalty through consistency of care rather than excitement.

The Caregiver's voice is warm, reassuring, and patient. It does not rush the audience. It does not sell. It serves. The Caregiver brand communicates, above all else: you are not alone in this.

The risk is being taken for granted or perceived as weak. The Caregiver that never asserts a point of view can become invisible. The best Caregiver brands combine genuine compassion with quiet confidence. They are not doormats. They are trusted.

Brands that live here: Johnson & Johnson, Allstate, Cleveland Clinic, Dove, TOMS.

The Creator

"Make your mark."

The Creator is driven by the need to build something that didn't exist before. This archetype is the engine of imagination. The Creator brand does not want to give its audience a finished product. It wants to give them the tools, materials, and inspiration to make something of their own. The Creator's relationship with its audience is a collaboration. Both are in the business of making.

The Creator's voice is expressive, generous with ideas, and genuinely excited about what is possible. It talks about craft. It honors the process. It celebrates things that are made well and made with intention.

The risk is perfectionism. The Creator brand that is so invested in quality that it becomes precious, precious about process, about collaboration, about what is "worthy" of the brand, can become inaccessible. The best Creator brands are inclusive. The invitation is open.

Brands that live here: Adobe, LEGO, Figma, YouTube, Etsy.

The Ruler

"Take control."

The Ruler creates order from chaos. This archetype is about authority, leadership, and the responsibility that comes with power. The Ruler brand does not ask for trust. It earns it, through expertise, through excellence, through a track record of delivering on what it promises at the highest possible standard. The Ruler's audience is people who demand the best and are willing to pay for it.

The Ruler's voice is authoritative, precise, and unhurried. It does not need to convince you it is the best. It knows it is. The best Ruler brands carry their confidence like a well-cut suit: effortless, earned, and immediately recognizable.

The risk is arrogance or rigidity. The Ruler that cannot adapt, that treats its authority as divine right rather than earned responsibility, eventually loses its crown. The best Ruler brands combine high standards with genuine accountability.

Brands that live here: Mercedes-Benz, Rolex, American Express, IBM, McKinsey.

THE BELONGING FAMILY

The Everyperson. The Sage. The Innocent.

Belonging-family archetypes offer acceptance, wisdom, and the comfort of the familiar. Their audiences are people who are tired of performing, who want to be seen for who they actually are, who are looking for something trustworthy, honest, and genuinely good. These brands do not ask you to be more. They meet you where you are. That is rarer than it sounds, and it earns a loyalty that is quieter but remarkably durable.

The Everyperson

"Just like you."

The Everyperson is the antidote to aspiration. Not because aspiration is bad, but because not everyone wants to be inspired to be more every time they interact with a brand. Sometimes people want to feel recognized, not elevated. The Everyperson brand says: we know you. We are you. No pretense, no performance, no velvet rope.

The Everyperson's voice is plain, warm, and honest. It uses simple words. It makes no reference to how sophisticated or innovative or disruptive it is. It just shows up and does what it promises.

The risk is disappearing into the middle. The Everyperson brand that is so committed to being unremarkable that it loses its identity entirely becomes furniture: useful, necessary, invisible. The best Everyperson brands have a genuine warmth and a specific point of view, even within their accessibility.

Brands that live here: IKEA, Target, Costco, Lyft, Cracker Barrel.

The Sage

"Truth over trend. Clarity over chaos."

The Sage knows. Not in a flashy, provocative way. In a steady, certain, quietly powerful way. The Sage brand has done the work, developed the expertise, earned the right to be believed, and now shares what it knows with clarity and without agenda. The Sage's audience is people who are overwhelmed by information and desperately want someone they can trust to tell them what is actually true.

The Sage's voice is measured, precise, and authoritative without being condescending. It is never the loudest in the room. It does not need to be. When the Sage speaks, people stop and listen because the Sage has earned that attention over time.

The risk is arrogance or inaccessibility. The Sage that speaks only to people who already agree, or that makes the audience feel uninformed rather than enlightened, loses its gift. The best Sage brands make complexity feel navigable. They do not make you feel dumb. They make you feel like you can understand, if you are willing to engage.

Brands that live here: Google, TED, The Economist, Harvard Business Review, Mayo Clinic.

The Innocent

"Keep it simple. Keep it good."

The Innocent believes the world can be exactly as good as it looks. This archetype is not naive. It is principled. The Innocent brand is committed to a version of the world where products do what they say, companies tell the truth, and goodness is its own reward. The Innocent's audience is people who are exhausted by cynicism and ready to believe in something uncomplicated.

The Innocent's voice is clear, optimistic, and unpretentious. It does not oversell. It does not need to. Its entire premise is that the thing is good and speaks for itself.

The risk is irrelevance in a complicated world. The Innocent brand that cannot acknowledge difficulty or nuance can feel out of touch. The best Innocent brands hold their optimism with awareness. They know the world is complicated. They choose to respond to it with clarity and goodness anyway. That choice is the brand.

Brands that live here: Innocent Drinks, Aveeno, Dove (in certain campaigns), Patagonia (environmental messaging), Warby Parker.

Finding Yours: The Field Assessment

Now that you have read all 12, here is what to do.

Do not overthink this. The archetype that is right for your brand is usually the one that felt most obvious while you were reading. The one where you thought: well, obviously. The ones that felt clearly wrong are also valuable information.

Work through these four questions. Write your answers. Do not edit while you write.

Question 1: The instinct question.

Which archetype description made you feel the most immediate recognition? Not "I aspire to this." Recognition. The feeling of: that is us.

Question 2: The evidence question.

Think about the moments when your brand was most itself. The best piece of content you made. The customer story you tell most often. The way your team behaves when things get hard. Which archetype shows up in those moments?

Question 3: The audience question.

Who buys from you and stays? Not your total addressable market. The people who become actual advocates, who tell other people, who come back. What do they have in common? Which archetype speaks to what they actually want?

Question 4: The elimination question.

Which archetype is most definitively not you? Eliminate anything that requires your brand to perform an identity it does not actually have. The ones left are your real candidates.

Most people end up with one clear primary and one secondary that adds texture. If you end up with three or more that all feel equally right, that is a signal that your brand has not yet committed to an identity. That is not a flaw. It is the reason you are reading this book.

On Blending Archetypes

This comes up every time, so let's address it directly.

Can a brand blend archetypes? Yes. Does it work? Sometimes. Under specific conditions.

The rule is this: one primary, one secondary, and the secondary serves the primary. It does not compete with it.

Patagonia is an Explorer brand with strong Rebel undertones. The exploration is primary. The rebellion against corporate environmental destruction is what gives the Explorer a mission rather than just a direction. The secondary archetype deepens the primary. It doesn't divide it.

Red Bull is a Hero brand with Jester energy. The heroism is primary: athletes pushing limits, human beings doing the impossible. The Jester energy shows up in the marketing's willingness to be absurd and self-aware. The wings campaign. The cartoons. The Jester keeps the Hero from taking itself too seriously. The secondary keeps the primary from becoming a cliche.

The combination that never works: two primary archetypes of equal weight. The Ruler and the Everyperson. The Hero and the Innocent. The Rebel and the Caregiver. These pairings create contradiction, not depth. The audience cannot reconcile them. They stop trying and move on.

You have one primary archetype. Claim it. A secondary can come later, once you know the primary cold.

The Brand That Tried to Be Everyone

Before we go into the deep dives in Chapter 3, one more thing.

You have seen this brand. You have probably worked with this brand or for this brand. Maybe you are this brand right now.

It is bold and trustworthy. Innovative and approachable. Premium and accessible. Disruptive and reliable. Expert and humble. Its brand guidelines contain nine values and a personality spectrum so wide it encompasses all possible temperatures of human response.

It tries to speak to everyone because it is afraid to speak to someone specific and lose the others.

What it actually does is speak clearly to no one.

Every archetype in the system is a specific kind of person with a specific kind of voice and a specific relationship with the audience. Trying to be three or four of them simultaneously is not versatility. It is identity confusion. And audiences, who are making gut-level decisions faster than they can articulate, feel that confusion immediately. They do not know what to make of you. So they make nothing of you.

The most powerful brand move you can make is specificity. Be one thing. Be it completely. Be it in every decision, every piece of content, every hire, every product choice, every customer service interaction.

The right people will find you. The wrong people will self-select out. That is not failure. That is the system working.

Now let's go deep.

Next: Chapter 3. The 12 Archetypes, Deep Dives.

This is where we open the portraits fully: character, voice, visual world, brand examples, red flags, exercises, and activation dares. One full chapter. Twelve full treatments.

CHAPTER 3:
Meet the 12: Deep Dives

"Until you make the unconscious conscious, it will direct your life and you will call it fate."

-- Carl Jung

This is the chapter you will return to.

Not just once while you are building your brand. Again when you are hiring. Again when a campaign is not landing. Again when someone on your team writes something and it sounds like a stranger wrote it. This chapter is a reference. Keep it close.

Each of the 12 archetypes gets its full portrait here: the character, four defining traits, the voice in action, the visual world, real brand examples, the conditions under which claiming this archetype makes sense, the honest red flags, a brand voice exercise, and an activation dare.

Read your archetype all the way through. Then read the ones adjacent to it. Then, if you are brave, read the one that feels most wrong for you. That one will teach you something too.

THE FREEDOM FAMILY

THE REBEL

"Rules were made to be broken."

The Character

The Rebel does not just push back against the rules. The Rebel believes the rules are the problem. Not out of nihilism. Out of conviction. The Rebel has looked at the existing order and decided that it serves the wrong people, protects the wrong things, and punishes the ones who should be free.

This is the archetype of liberation through defiance. The Rebel brand does not ask permission. It acts. It disrupts categories, challenges norms, and gives its audience something they did not know they were allowed to want: a brand that refuses to play the game everyone else is playing.

The Rebel is magnetic because it says out loud what its audience has been thinking quietly. It voices the frustration, the restlessness, the refusal to accept things as they are. In doing so, it creates an instant us-versus-them dynamic. Not enemies in any harmful sense. But a clear line between those who get it and those who do not. The Rebel's audience loves being on the right side of that line.

The danger is that Rebel energy without genuine conviction becomes theater. The brand that performs rebellion without actually standing for anything will be found out. Audiences can tell the difference between a brand that disrupts because it has to and one that disrupts because it wants to look edgy. The first earns loyalty. The second earns eye rolls.

Four Defining Traits

Defiant. The Rebel brand says no to things other brands say yes to. Categories, conventions, aesthetics, pricing structures, distribution norms. Defiance is not the strategy. It is the character expressing itself.

Provocative. The Rebel does not traffic in comfortable messaging. It says things that make certain people uncomfortable. That is intentional. The discomfort filters the audience down to exactly the right people.

Liberating. The Rebel does not just rebel for its own sake. It rebels on behalf of its audience. The underlying message is always: you do not have to accept the version of this that everyone else accepts. There is another way.

Loyal to its tribe. The Rebel brand draws a line and stands on one side of it. The people who stand on the same side become fiercely loyal. The Rebel does not try to move them. It belongs to them.

The Voice in Action

Rebel copy is short. Declarative. It does not explain itself at length because it does not feel the need to justify its existence to anyone who would require that much convincing.

It uses plain language. Not formal. Not corporate. Street-level. The Rebel voice sounds like someone who has no patience for marketing language because they see through it.

It is comfortable with tension. It will say something that makes a portion of the audience uncomfortable, and it will not follow it with a softening qualifier.

Sounds like:

"We're not for everyone. Good."

"They said it couldn't be done. They were wrong. Again."

"Everything they told you about this category is a sales pitch. Here's the truth."

"Built for people who don't fit in boxes."

Does not sound like:

"We're committed to delivering innovative solutions…"

"Our award-winning team..."

"Trusted by thousands of customers..."

The Visual World

Raw over refined. Black, deep red, industrial grays. Texture that suggests wear. Typography that feels handmade or brutally simple, never decorative. Photography that captures movement, grit, real environments. Not studio shots of happy people. Real moments with real edges.

The Rebel visual world signals: we did not hire a brand agency to make this feel safe. This is what we actually are.

Brand Examples

Harley-Davidson. The original Rebel brand in the consumer market. Not because their motorcycles are the most powerful or the most technologically advanced. Because riding a Harley is a declaration. The brand built an entire culture around the freedom to be exactly who you are regardless of what anyone thinks.

BrewDog. Started as two guys and a dog brewing beer in a garage in Scotland, explicitly positioned against what they called "the bland, corporate beer world." Their early marketing was confrontational, deliberately provocative, and deeply effective. They grew a global brand on the back of Rebel conviction.

Liquid Death. Sells water. In tallboy cans. With death metal branding. On the surface absurd. Underneath it, a precise Rebel move: taking the most boring category in beverages and murdering the convention so thoroughly that the brand became more interesting than most alcohol companies.

Challenger brand example: Any independent restaurant group that openly mocks the chain restaurant experience, any tech company that names the incumbent as the enemy in its positioning, any agency that publishes a manifesto about why most agencies are broken.

Claim This Archetype If...

Your brand was genuinely built as a response to something wrong with the existing options. You have actual conviction, not just attitude. Your team embodies the rebellion, not just your marketing. You are comfortable with the segment of the market that will never buy from you because you are not for them. Your product or service actually delivers on the liberation it promises.

Red Flags

You are using Rebel language because it seems to get attention, not because your brand actually stands for something transgressive. Your leadership wants to be provocative in marketing but conservative in every other decision. You are targeting everyone and hoping the edgy voice will differentiate you. Your Rebel positioning is not matched by your actual behavior as a company.

Brand Voice Exercise

Write three things your brand believes that your category does not want to say out loud. The things that, if a competitor read them, they would be uncomfortable. Not because they are mean. Because they are true. That list is your Rebel voice waiting to be used.

Activation Dare

Publish a piece of content that takes a direct, named position against a category convention or norm. Not a vague "we do things differently." A specific, clear statement of what you think is wrong with the way things are done and why you built something different. Watch who responds.

I'll do it now. "Driverless cars delivering your tacos is stupid. Use Doordash and support a human person in your local community."

THE EXPLORER

"Go your own way."

The Character

The Explorer is driven by a hunger that cannot be satisfied by anything familiar. New terrain. New ideas. New experiences. New versions of what is possible. The Explorer brand exists to push past the edges of the known world and to bring its audience along for the journey.

This is not recklessness. The best Explorer brands are deeply prepared for the territory they enter. They respect the wilderness. They know the gear, know the risks, and go anyway because the pull of what is undiscovered is stronger than the comfort of the known.

The Explorer's relationship with its audience is one of invitation. Not instruction. The Explorer does not tell its audience where to go. It opens doors and says: there is more out there. Go see. The Explorer brand gives people permission to follow their own curiosity, to break from the prescribed path, to trust that what they find at the edge of the map will be worth the journey.

The Explorer carries a particular kind of authenticity requirement. More than almost any other archetype, the Explorer brand must actually live what it preaches. An Explorer brand that is run from a corporate headquarters by people who have never used the product in the field, never taken the risk, never gotten mud on their boots, will be sniffed out immediately by exactly the audience it is trying to reach.

Four Defining Traits

Curious. The Explorer is never satisfied with the explanation it already has. There is always another question, another angle, another layer of the territory to understand. That curiosity is visible in how the brand communicates.

Independent. The Explorer does not follow. It is comfortable going in a direction nobody else has validated yet. The Explorer brand takes positions before consensus forms, makes moves before the market confirms them, trusts its own sense of direction.

Honest about the difficulty. The Explorer does not pretend the journey is easy. It acknowledges the hardship, the uncertainty, the moments where the path disappears. That honesty is part of the respect the Explorer has for its audience.

Horizon-oriented. The Explorer is always looking ahead. There is energy and forward momentum to the Explorer brand. It never feels settled. It feels like there is always somewhere further to go.

The Voice in Action

Explorer copy breathes. It has space in it. It is not in a hurry to close the deal because the Explorer is not primarily about closing. It is about opening.

It asks questions more than it makes declarations. It describes experiences rather than features. It uses geographic and sensory language: terrain, distance, light, texture, depth.

The Explorer voice does not oversell. It does not need to. The invitation is enough.

Sounds like:

"There's a version of this nobody has seen yet. We're going to find it."

"The best route is the one nobody's mapped."

"We don't know exactly what's out there. That's why we're going."

"Built for the people who want to know what's around the next corner."

Does not sound like:

"The industry-leading solution for your needs."

"Optimized for maximum performance."

"Join millions of satisfied customers."

The Visual World

Open space. Natural light. Real environments. Horizon lines. Photography that conveys distance and scale, that makes the viewer feel small in a good way. Color palettes borrowed from the earth: slate, forest, ochre, granite. Typography that is functional, durable, legible under duress.

The Explorer's visual world does not perform beauty. It discovers it.

Brand Examples

Patagonia. The gold standard Explorer brand. Their products are made for the places most people never go. Their marketing looks like expedition documentation. Their environmental mission gives the exploration a purpose beyond recreation. Patagonia does not sell gear. It sells the belief that the wild world is worth protecting and worth entering.

REI. Every product category, one invitation: go outside. The #OptOutside campaign, in which REI closed on Black Friday and paid its employees to go outdoors instead, is one of the cleanest Explorer brand moves in recent memory. It cost them one day of retail revenue. It earned them years of cultural credibility.

Airbnb. The original pitch was pure Explorer: do not stay in a hotel. Stay in someone's home. Belong anywhere. The Explorer archetype is embedded in the founding premise.

National Geographic. The world is more extraordinary than you know. Let us show you. That sentence is National Geographic's entire brand identity, and it has been for over a century.

Claim This Archetype If...

Your brand genuinely pushes into territory others have not entered. Your founders have the Explorer instinct personally. The journey your customer takes with your product is itself part of the value. Your audience is defined more by curiosity and independence than by demographics. You have a genuine point of view about what conventional wisdom gets wrong about your space.

Red Flags

Your Explorer positioning is aspirational imagery with no substance behind it. The "exploration" your brand references is metaphorical to the point of meaninglessness. Your audience is actually risk-averse and looking for safety, not adventure. Your brand voice says Explorer but your company culture says stay in your lane.

Brand Voice Exercise

Describe your product or service as if you are writing a field report from somewhere no one has been before. What did you find there? What is different about this territory than people expect? What does the audience need to know before they enter? Write it as a dispatch, not a pitch.

Activation Dare

Find the thing in your category that everyone accepts as a given and question it publicly. Not "we do things differently." The specific assumption. The specific convention. The specific received wisdom that your brand, through its own exploration, has found to be wrong or incomplete. Publish that. That is Explorer content.

THE MAGICIAN

"Turn insight into alchemy."

The Character

The Magician sees what others cannot see and does what others believe cannot be done. This archetype lives at the intersection of vision and execution. The Magician brand does not just have ideas. It transforms them into reality. And in doing so, it transforms the people and the world around it.

The Magician operates with a sense of wonder that it does not try to explain away. There is mystery here, intentional mystery. The Magician understands that some things are more powerful when they are felt than when they are explained. The best Magician brands create experiences that feel like they should not be possible and then let the audience sit in that feeling before offering any rational account of how it happened.

The Magician's audience wants transformation. Not improvement. Not incremental gain. Transformation. They want to hand something over to the Magician and receive back something qualitatively different. Better in a way that changes what they believe is possible.

The Magician carries enormous responsibility. The power to transform implies the power to deceive. The Magician that overpromises and underdelivers does not just disappoint. It betrays. The trust the Magician earns through wonder is the most valuable trust there is, and the fastest to collapse.

Four Defining Traits

Visionary. The Magician sees the future more clearly than the present. It does not describe what is. It describes what will be, once the transformation is complete.

Transformational. The Magician brand's promise is change. Not minor improvement. Real change. The before and after are qualitatively different.

Intuitive. The Magician trusts instinct over data. It makes moves that cannot be fully rationalized at the moment they are made and is proven right after the fact.

Purposeful. The best Magician brands transform toward something. The magic is in service of a larger vision. Without purpose, the Magician becomes a trickster.

The Voice in Action

Magician copy is evocative and precise at once. It uses language that creates pictures, that makes the abstract feel visceral, that lets you feel the transformation before it happens. But it is not vague. It paints a specific picture of a specific possibility.

The Magician voice does not explain the mechanism. It describes the outcome. The wonder is preserved by not dismantling it.

Sounds like:

"This changes everything."

"You won't believe this is possible until you see it."

"The future arrived earlier than expected."

"We made the impossible table stakes."

Does not sound like:

"Our proprietary algorithm delivers..."

"Step-by-step results you can measure."

"Trusted by experts in the field."

The Visual World

Sleek, minimal, intentional. Every element in the frame is there on purpose. Dark backgrounds that make the product glow. Light that feels almost theatrical. White space used as a design element, not a placeholder. Motion that feels choreographed. Typography that is confident and clean.

The Magician's visual world says: everything you are about to experience was considered carefully.

Brand Examples

Apple. The definitive Magician brand. From "Think Different" to "One more thing," Apple has consistently delivered the experience of witnessing the impossible become real. The product launches are rituals. The unboxing is a ceremony. The Magician archetype is not in Apple's marketing. It is in every decision the company makes about how its products look, feel, and work.

Disney. A hundred years of transforming stories into experiences that make adults cry and children believe. Disney's core Magician promise has not changed: we will take you somewhere that is not real and make it feel realer than real.

Tesla. The early Tesla brand was pure Magician. Electric cars that were slow and impractical? The Magician would like a word. The Model S changed what the audience believed was possible. The subsequent brand evolution has complicated the archetype, but the founding energy was unmistakably Magician.

Challenger brand example: Any design tool, AI product, or creative platform that genuinely does something the user did not believe software could do. The Magician is alive everywhere genuine transformation happens.

Claim This Archetype If...

Your product or service genuinely produces results that surprise people. Your founding story involves seeing a possibility that the market had dismissed. You have a vision of a transformed world, not just a better version of the current one. Your audience's primary desire is transformation, not just improvement.

Red Flags

Your "magic" is mostly aesthetic. The transformation you promise is incremental improvement dressed in visionary language. Your brand overpromises and your product underdelivers. Your team is better at creating wonder than sustaining it through execution.

Brand Voice Exercise

Write a description of what your customer's world looks like after they have experienced your brand. Not what your product does. What their life, work, or business looks like on the other side. Make it specific. Make it feel possible and slightly miraculous at the same time.

Activation Dare

Find one thing your brand does that nobody in your category does and build a piece of content entirely around the transformation it produces. No features. No specs. No comparison charts. Just the before, the moment of transformation, and the after. Let the result do the work.

THE SOCIAL FAMILY

THE HERO

"Challenge accepted."

The Character

The Hero does not know if they will win. They go anyway.

This is the essential truth of the Hero archetype: it is not about certainty or invincibility. It is about the willingness to face what is hard, to show up for the challenge when everything rational says to stay home, and to discover in the process that you were capable of more than you knew.

The Hero brand believes in its audience. Not in a soft, supportive way. In a demanding, respectful way. The Hero brand says: you have something in you. We are going to help you find it. And finding it is going to require work, discomfort, and the willingness to fail before you succeed.

The Hero's relationship with its audience is built on shared struggle. The Hero brand does not stand above the fight looking down. It is in the fight with you, believing in what you can do, refusing to let you accept a smaller version of what you are capable of.

The Hero brand works in any category where the customer faces genuine challenge: physical, professional, creative, emotional. The common thread is not the nature of the challenge. It is the posture toward it.

Four Defining Traits

Courageous. The Hero does not wait for conditions to be perfect. It moves. It acts. It takes the risk.

Driven. There is an engine in the Hero that does not switch off. The mission is not complete. The challenge is not resolved. There is always more to do and the Hero is ready to do it.

Disciplined. The Hero earns its wins. It does not cut corners. It believes in the process even when the process is painful.

Inspiring. The Hero brand makes its audience believe in their own potential. That belief is the product, as much as anything tangible.

The Voice in Action

Hero copy is active. Every verb is doing work. Short sentences. Forward momentum. The Hero voice does not look back. It does not dwell. It moves.

It respects the struggle without romanticizing it. The Hero acknowledges that the thing you are doing is hard. Then it tells you to do it anyway.

Sounds like:

"Just do it."

"Earn it."

"The only way out is through."

"You were built for this."

"Winning isn't everything. Trying is."

Does not sound like:

"We make the process easier so you don't have to..."

"Sit back and let us handle it."

"Stress-free. Effortless. Automatic."

The Visual World

Kinetic. Bodies in motion. Sweat. Effort visible in faces and posture. Real athletes, real workers, real people doing difficult things. High contrast.

Strong light. Colors that are bold and uncomplicated: black, white, primary colors at full saturation.

The Hero's visual world says: this is what it looks like to try.

Brand Examples

Nike. Forty years of the same Hero promise, delivered in ten thousand different ways. The product is fine. The archetype is extraordinary. "Just Do It" is the Hero's thesis statement in three words.

Under Armour. The Hero with a chip on its shoulder. Where Nike is the established champion, Under Armour built its brand on the underdog's determination. "I Will" is the Hero's personal manifesto.

Peloton. The Hero archetype applied to home fitness. The instructors are Heroes. The leaderboard makes you one. The entire product experience is designed to make you feel that the work you are doing means something.

Gatorade. As noted in Chapter 1, the textbook uses Gatorade as a marketing mix example. What the textbook does not say is that Gatorade is a Hero brand. The electrolytes are real. The sweat is real. But what keeps Gatorade dominant against dozens of competitors with similar formulas is the Hero archetype running through everything they make. The athlete. The challenge. The push through.

Claim This Archetype If...

Your product helps people accomplish something difficult. Your audience is goal-oriented and motivated by achievement. Your brand genuinely believes in the capacity of its customers to rise to challenges. Your team embodies the Hero's work ethic internally. You are not afraid of demanding things from your audience.

Red Flags

Your brand uses Hero language but your product is actually about making things easier and reducing effort. Your audience is not motivated by challenge; they are motivated by comfort and convenience. Your messaging is all inspiration with nothing to back it up. You confuse the Hero archetype with machismo or aggression.

Brand Voice Exercise

Write the speech your brand would give to a customer who is about to give up. Not a sales pitch. The real talk. The thing you would say if you genuinely believed in them. That speech is your Hero voice.

Activation Dare

Find a real customer who used your product or service to accomplish something genuinely hard. Tell their story. Not as a testimonial. As a Hero's journey. The struggle, the turning point, the win. Run it everywhere.

THE LOVER

"Feel something."

The Character

The Lover is the archetype of desire: the desire for beauty, for connection, for pleasure, for the experience of being fully present in a moment that is worth savoring. The Lover brand does not sell products. It sells experiences. It does not optimize for utility. It optimizes for feeling.

The Lover understands something that more rational archetypes miss: humans are sensory beings before they are logical ones. The right smell, the right texture, the right sound in the right moment can produce feelings that no amount of feature optimization can touch. The Lover brand operates at the level of the senses and invests in those experiences the way other brands invest in specs.

The Lover's relationship with its audience is intimate. Not in any inappropriate sense. In the sense that the Lover sees the audience. It knows what they desire. It honors that desire rather than managing it. The Lover brand makes people feel worthy of something extraordinary.

The Lover archetype is not limited to luxury goods or romance categories. It lives anywhere genuine desire exists: the perfect meal, the perfect running playlist, the room that is exactly right, the tool that fits perfectly in the hand. The Lover is about the experience of quality from the inside.

Four Defining Traits

Sensory. The Lover brand invests in the texture of the experience: how it smells, sounds, feels, tastes. Every touchpoint is considered for how it will land in the body, not just the mind.

Intimate. The Lover speaks one-on-one. Even when it is communicating at scale, the Lover voice feels like it is written for one person. The audience feels seen and chosen.

Passionate. The Lover is not moderate about anything. It believes in what it offers with an intensity that is contagious.

Devoted. The Lover brand does not abandon its audience after the sale. It tends the relationship. It shows up with care and attention over time.

The Voice in Action

Lover copy is rich and unhurried. It takes time with language the way a fine meal takes time at the table. It uses sensory words: texture, warmth, depth, richness. It does not bullet point. It flows.

The Lover voice never feels like it is trying to close you. It is not in a hurry. The experience of reading it should itself be pleasurable.

Sounds like:

"Made for the moment you want to remember."

"Some things deserve more than a few seconds of your attention."

"Crafted for the ones who feel everything."

"This is what it's supposed to taste like."

Does not sound like:

"High-performance formula with maximum efficiency."

"Get more done in less time."

"Trusted by professionals worldwide."

The Visual World

Lush. Warm. Intimate. Photography that lingers: close-ups of texture, light falling at the right angle, people in genuine moments of pleasure rather than posed enthusiasm. Color palettes that are rich and considered: deep jewel tones, warm neutrals, the particular shade of light just before sunset.

The Lover's visual world says: slow down. There is something here worth attending to.

Brand Examples

Chanel. The Lover brand built into a fashion empire. Every element of the Chanel experience, from the packaging to the store environment to the fragrance advertising, is designed to make the audience feel that they have entered a world where beauty and desire are taken seriously.

Häagen-Dazs. Ice cream positioned not as a treat but as an experience of pleasure. The typography, the flavor names, the advertising (a couple sharing a spoonful late at night): all Lover.

Bose. Sound is intimate. Bose built an entire brand around the idea that music heard properly is a sensory experience worth investing in. Their noise-canceling headphone campaigns are Lover brand work: the world disappears and there is only you and the music.

Challenger brand example: Any food and beverage brand built around ritual and occasion rather than convenience. Any skincare brand that takes the act of caring for yourself seriously as a form of self-love.

Claim This Archetype If...

Your product is designed to be experienced, not just used. Pleasure, beauty, or connection is central to what your brand delivers. Your audience makes decisions based on how something makes them feel as much as what it does. Your team cares deeply about the quality of the experience, not just the quality of the output.

Red Flags

Your Lover positioning is all aesthetics with no substance. The experience you promise does not match the experience you deliver. Your brand uses intimacy as a marketing device rather than as a genuine expression of how you feel about your audience. You are in a category where decisions are made rationally and your Lover positioning confuses rather than connects.

Brand Voice Exercise

Describe your product without mentioning what it does. Describe only how it feels to use it. The sensory experience. The emotional resonance. The moment it creates. That description is your Lover voice.

Activation Dare

Create a piece of content that slows down. Not a 30-second ad. Not a carousel. Something that takes its time: a long-form piece, a film, a series of images that build. Something that treats the audience as people who deserve more than a quick scroll. See who stays.

THE JESTER

"Serious brands are seriously boring."

The Character

The Jester knows a secret that most brands are too afraid to use: laughter is one of the most powerful forces in human connection. Not cheap laughter, not mean laughter, but the genuine, disarming, coffee-out-of-the-nose kind of laughter that breaks down walls and creates instant intimacy.

The Jester is not silly for the sake of it. The Jester is honest in the way that only humor allows. Comedy requires truth. The funniest things are always the truest things, the observations that make people laugh and then immediately think: I have never heard anyone say that but I have always known it. The Jester brand tells those truths. In doing so, it creates a connection that the serious archetypes spend years building.

The Jester's audience is not looking for inspiration or wisdom or transformation. They are looking to be delighted. They are tired of being marketed at and they are grateful for any brand that appears to know how ridiculous all of this is. The Jester brand gives them that.

The Jester archetype is perhaps the most dangerous to execute badly. Comedy that lands is magic. Comedy that does not land is a disaster. The Jester brand must be genuinely funny, which means it must take humor seriously as a craft and commit fully. Half-hearted Jester energy is worse than no Jester energy at all.

Four Defining Traits

Playful. The Jester does not take itself seriously. It can laugh at itself. It can find the absurdity in its own existence and point at it with affection.

Honest. The Jester's humor is almost always truth-delivery in disguise. The jokes are funny because they are true. The brand is trusted because it says what everyone is thinking.

Quick. The Jester moves fast. It responds to the moment. The best Jester brand content feels like someone was watching the world and reacted faster and funnier than anyone else.

Irreverent. The Jester has no sacred cows. Nothing is too important to make fun of, including the brand itself. That irreverence is part of the charm.

The Voice in Action

Jester copy is fast, sharp, and unexpected. The best Jester sentences have a turn in them: they set up one expectation and deliver something else. They play with language. They surprise.

The Jester voice is unafraid to be weird. It is unafraid to be absurd. It is unafraid to go somewhere the brand guidelines definitely did not anticipate.

Sounds like:

"Water for people who are dead inside. (And outside.)"

"We started because we thought our company's marketing was garbage. Now it's your problem."

"Our competitors have awards. We have your attention."

"Probably the best beer in the world. Probably."

Does not sound like:

"We are excited to announce..."

"Our team is passionate about..."

"Delivering excellence in every interaction."

The Visual World

Unexpected. Irreverent. Often deliberately lo-fi as a statement against over-produced brand aesthetics. Color choices that are surprising or deliberately wrong in a right way. Typography that plays. Illustration over photography when illustration can be stranger and more specific. The Jester's visual world says: we made this with a sense of humor and we are not apologizing for it.

Brand Examples

Old Spice. "The Man Your Man Could Smell Like" was a piece of work so strange and so confident that it revived a dying brand. The Jester archetype used with full commitment: absurdist, fast-moving, impossible to look away from.

Liquid Death. Mentioned in the Rebel section as well, because Liquid Death is doing something genuinely interesting: it is running Jester and Rebel simultaneously as primary archetypes in an unusual combination that seems to work because both archetypes are in service of the same audience truth.

Dollar Shave Club. "Our blades are f*ing great." One video. Entire brand built. Pure Jester: honest, fast, irreverent, and underneath the humor, a completely clear value proposition.

Duolingo. The social media version of Duolingo is one of the best Jester brand executions in recent memory. The app is earnest and educational. The social media presence is chaotic, threatening, and genuinely funny. The dissonance is the point.

Claim This Archetype If...

Your team is genuinely funny, not just funny in meetings. You have the courage to be weird in public. Your audience has a sense of humor about the category they are in. You can sustain genuine comedic execution over time, not just launch with one funny video and then revert to corporate.

Red Flags

You want to be funny but your leadership is not actually comfortable with what funny requires. Your humor is safe, committee-approved, and therefore not funny. Your category demands a level of trust and seriousness that the Jester undermines. You are using humor as a substitute for substance rather than as a vehicle for it.

Brand Voice Exercise

Pick the most boring, corporate-sounding sentence in your current brand messaging. Rewrite it four times: each time funnier and more irreverent than the last. The fourth version is probably closer to your real Jester voice than anything in your current brand guidelines.

Activation Dare

Find the funniest, most honest thing that could be said about your category, your product, or your brand, and say it. Publicly. In the format where you have the most visibility. Do not soften it. The discomfort before you post is the Jester voice. That is the one.

THE ORDER FAMILY

THE CAREGIVER

"We've got you."

The Character

The Caregiver shows up. That is the simplest and most complete description of this archetype. When things are hard, when the audience needs something, when there is a gap between where someone is and where they need to be: the Caregiver closes it.

The Caregiver brand is not motivated by transaction. It is motivated by genuine concern for the people it serves. The Caregiver does not ask what it can sell. It asks what it can do. That orientation, which sounds simple and is actually rare, is the source of enormous loyalty.

The Caregiver's relationship with its audience is built on trust earned through consistency. Not on a dramatic promise or a transformative claim. On showing up, reliably, over time. The Caregiver brand is the one you call when something goes wrong. The one you know will pick up. The one that has never given you a reason to doubt it.

The Caregiver is often underestimated as an archetype because it is not flashy. It does not disrupt. It does not transform. It protects and serves, quietly and persistently, and those qualities are harder to build and more durable than almost anything else in the archetype system.

Four Defining Traits

Empathetic. The Caregiver understands what the audience is going through from the inside. Not as an analysis. As a genuine emotional resonance.

Reliable. The Caregiver is there. Every time. That consistency is not a feature. It is the entire brand promise.

Selfless. The Caregiver brand prioritizes the audience's needs over its own agenda. The customer's experience comes first, even when that is inconvenient.

Protective. The Caregiver stands between its audience and the things that can hurt them. That protective instinct is expressed in product design, service delivery, and communication.

The Voice in Action

Caregiver copy is warm and direct. It does not perform empathy with overwrought language. It demonstrates it by being clear, honest, and genuinely useful. The Caregiver voice does not sell. It helps.

It uses "you" more than any other pronoun. It is relentlessly about the audience, not the brand.

Sounds like:

"We've got you."

"You don't have to handle this alone."

"Whatever you need. Whenever you need it."

"We think about you when things are good. We're there when they're not."

Does not sound like:

"Industry-leading innovation in..."

"Proud to be recognized as..."

"Disrupting the way care is delivered."

The Visual World

Warm. Human. Real faces in real moments. Not stock photography warmth. Genuine warmth. Soft light. Natural environments. The visual world of the Caregiver says: we see you as a person, not a market segment.

Brand Examples

Johnson & Johnson. Built the entire consumer brand on the Caregiver: gentle products for people at their most vulnerable, babies and patients and families managing difficulty.

Allstate. "You're in good hands." Four words. The entirety of the Caregiver brand promise. The protective instinct made into a tagline.

Dove. The Real Beauty campaign was Caregiver work: a brand standing up for its audience against the industry standards that were harming them.

Cleveland Clinic. One of the best healthcare Caregiver brands. Their content marketing is built around genuine patient stories, medical education, and the orientation that the patient comes first.

Claim This Archetype If...

Your brand was built to solve a real problem that affects people in meaningful ways. Your team genuinely cares about the outcomes for your customers, not just the transaction. Your product or service is used during moments of vulnerability or significant need. Consistency and reliability are the qualities that drive loyalty in your category.

Red Flags

Your brand uses Caregiver language but your service delivery does not back it up. You perform empathy in your marketing while making it difficult for customers to actually get help. Your organization is optimized for internal efficiency over customer experience. The Caregiver mask slips any time there is a cost or inconvenience involved.

Brand Voice Exercise

Write a response to a customer at their most frustrated, most confused, or most vulnerable moment with your product. Not the customer service script. The real response, the one that genuinely addresses what they need. That is your Caregiver voice at its clearest.

Activation Dare

Identify the most common moment of difficulty or confusion your customers face with your product or service. Build a piece of content, a guide, a video, a resource, that addresses it completely, with no sales agenda. Pure help. Publish it. See what happens to trust.

THE CREATOR

"Make your mark."

The Character

The Creator is driven by a compulsion that the other archetypes do not fully share: the need to make something that did not exist before. The Creator brand is not in the business of delivering what customers already know they want. It is in the business of enabling them to make what they could not previously imagine.

The Creator's relationship with its audience is fundamentally collaborative. The Creator brand does not complete the work for the audience. It gives them the tools, the materials, the inspiration, and the permission to complete it themselves. The Creator brand trusts its audience to make something worth making. That trust is reciprocated fiercely.

The Creator brand lives in categories where making is the experience. Software that enables creation. Tools for building. Platforms for expression. Educational products that develop skills. Communities built around craft. Any context where the audience is not a passive consumer but an active producer.

The Creator archetype is the one most closely aligned with the archetype this book was written in. Explorer and Creator share a horizon-orientation, a belief that the best things have not been made yet, and a respect for the process of making.

Four Defining Traits

Imaginative. The Creator brand sees possibility everywhere. It is always asking: what could this become? What else could be made with this?

Craft-oriented. The Creator has a reverence for quality and for the process of doing things well. Shortcuts are a betrayal of the work.

Expressive. The Creator brand has a distinctive point of view that comes through in everything it makes. It is not generic. It has voice and personality.

Empowering. The Creator's ultimate goal is to increase what its audience can make. The Creator brand succeeds when its customers make things they could not have made without it.

The Voice in Action

Creator copy is generous. It shares. It teaches. It celebrates what others make. The Creator voice does not hoard insight. It distributes it.

It is also specific. The Creator has opinions about the right way to do things. It does not hide those opinions behind false neutrality.

Sounds like:

"Make something that matters."

"The best work of your life is ahead of you."

"We didn't build this for passive users. We built it for makers."

"Your creativity is the point. Everything else is infrastructure."

Does not sound like:

"Automated for efficiency."

"No expertise required."

"Let our AI do the work for you."

The Visual World

The Creator's visual world celebrates the made thing. The work itself. Process shots. Tools. Materials. The moment of creation. Work shown in its real environment: the studio, the workshop, the desk covered in drafts. Typography that has personality and specificity. Color that is considered and intentional.

Brand Examples

Adobe. Forty years of the Creator archetype. The tools change. The brand promise does not: we make the tools that makers use to make everything else.

LEGO. Every set is an instruction, but the instruction is secondary to the invitation. The real LEGO message is: here are the bricks. Build something impossible. There is a reason LEGO survives every wave of digital entertainment. It is the purest Creator brand in the toy category.

Figma. Adobe for the next generation of digital creators. The Creator archetype in a platform built explicitly for the design process, not just the design output.

Etsy. A marketplace, but one that frames the transaction entirely around the maker. The seller is the hero. The product is a made thing with a story.

Claim This Archetype If...

Making is central to the experience your brand enables. Your audience self-identifies as creators, makers, builders, or artists in some form. The quality of what they make with your product matters to you as a measure of your own success. You have strong opinions about craft and quality that you are willing to express.

Red Flags

Your brand claims Creator positioning while actually reducing the need for human creativity. Your tools are designed for consumption, not creation. Your audience's primary goal is convenience and output, not the experience of making. Your Creator language is aspirational imagery with no actual creative enabling behind it.

Brand Voice Exercise

Write a celebration of something a customer made using your product. Not a testimonial. A genuine celebration of the work itself. What did they make? Why does it matter? How did you contribute to its existence? That piece is your Creator voice in action.

Activation Dare

Find the most interesting thing a customer has ever made with your product and showcase it as if it were a gallery opening. The full story. The process. The result. The maker. Not a case study. A tribute. See how other creators respond.

THE RULER

"Take control."

The Character

The Ruler does not ask for authority. It has earned it, through expertise, through consistency, through a standard of excellence that has proven itself over time. The Ruler brand does not position itself as premium. It defines what premium means in its category and holds that line.

The Ruler brand's audience wants the best and understands that the best costs more. They are not looking for a deal. They are looking for certainty: the certainty that what they are buying is the finest available version of the thing, that it will work the way it should, and that it will last. The Ruler brand delivers that certainty and maintains it without exception.

The Ruler operates with a kind of confidence that other archetypes approach but do not quite achieve. The Ruler is not trying to convince you. It does not need your validation. It sets the standard and invites those who meet it to belong.

The Ruler carries the heaviest responsibility in the archetype system. Because the Ruler positions itself as the authority, any failure, any inconsistency, any gap between the promise and the delivery is not a disappointment. It is a betrayal. The Ruler brand must be extraordinary in order to justify extraordinary positioning.

Four Defining Traits

Authoritative. The Ruler speaks from a position of earned expertise. It does not hedge. It does not qualify. It knows.

Responsible. Power without responsibility is tyranny. The best Ruler brands take genuine responsibility for the standard they have claimed. They own their failures and are public about their commitment to do better.

Precise. The Ruler is not approximate. In language, in design, in product quality: precision is a value.

Aspirational. The Ruler brand creates the desire to belong at the level it represents. People do not just want the product. They want what having the product means.

The Voice in Action

Ruler copy is spare and confident. It does not oversell because it does not need to. Every word is there on purpose. The Ruler voice is authoritative without being arrogant, which is a difficult balance that requires enormous discipline.

Sounds like:

"The best, or nothing."

"Not for everyone. For those who know."

"Excellence doesn't advertise itself. It demonstrates itself."

"This is what it looks like when no compromises are made."

Does not sound like:

"Affordable luxury for all."

"We believe everyone deserves…"

"Our friendly team is here to help."

The Visual World

Restrained. Precise. Every visual element is purposeful and high quality. White space used as a luxury signal. Typography chosen for authority and elegance. Photography that is technically perfect. Materials, if physical, that communicate quality through touch. The Ruler visual world says: nothing here was left to chance.

Brand Examples

Mercedes-Benz. "The best or nothing." Four words that encapsulate the Ruler archetype perfectly. Not the fastest. Not the most innovative. The best.

Rolex. A watch that keeps time, which all watches do. A Ruler brand that has made "Rolex" synonymous with achievement and permanence. The product is excellent. The archetype is why a Rolex is a statement.

American Express. Membership has its privileges. The Ruler brand applied to financial services. The Black Card is a Ruler symbol that has nothing to do with the card's actual features.

IBM. "Nobody ever got fired for buying IBM." The most honest Ruler brand line ever written. It speaks directly to the Ruler archetype's audience: people for whom certainty and authority are the purchasing criteria.

Claim This Archetype If...

Your product or service genuinely operates at the highest level in its category. Your audience makes decisions based on quality, authority, and prestige. You are willing to hold the line on standards even when it costs you business. Your organization has the internal culture of excellence to back up the external positioning.

Red Flags

You are using Ruler language for a mid-market product. Your quality is good but not genuinely the best. Your team is not aligned on a high standard of excellence in every function. You are positioning for prestige without the substance to sustain it.

Brand Voice Exercise

Write a description of your product as if you were explaining to a discerning audience why it is worth more than the alternatives. Not features. Standards. What do you refuse to compromise on, and why does that refusal matter? That is your Ruler voice.

Activation Dare

Publish your standards. Not your values, which every company has and which are largely identical. Your actual standards for what you will and will not do, make, ship, or say. The things you refuse to compromise on. The things that disqualify customers who are not the right fit. The things that define excellence in your world. That document is Ruler brand content.

THE BELONGING FAMILY

THE EVERYPERSON

"Just like you."

The Character

The Everyperson is the antidote to aspiration overload. In a world full of brands telling their audience to be more, do more, achieve more, the Everyperson says: you are already enough. Come as you are. No performance required.

The Everyperson brand builds trust through radical familiarity. Not by being impressive. By being recognizable. The audience sees themselves in the Everyperson brand, not a better version of themselves, just themselves. That recognition is powerful in a way that aspiration can never quite reach, because it does not require the audience to close any gap. It meets them where they are.

The Everyperson is easy to underestimate because its power is quiet. There are no dramatic transformations, no impossible feats, no moments of wonder. Just consistent, genuine, no-pretense showing up for the audience it serves.

The Everyperson archetype is hardest to execute well because it requires the brand to be genuinely unpretentious, which means the entire organization must resist the very human impulse to signal its own importance. Every time the Everyperson brand starts trying to be impressive, it loses what makes it work.

Four Defining Traits

Authentic. The Everyperson brand does not perform. What you see is what there is. The transparency is the feature.

Unpretentious. The Everyperson does not use jargon, does not emphasize prestige, does not position itself above its audience in any way.

Warm. The Everyperson brand is easy to be around. There is no intimidation factor. The relationship feels peer-to-peer.

Dependable. The Everyperson may not be the most exciting brand in the category. But it shows up. Every time. Without drama.

The Voice in Action

Everyperson copy is plain. Not dumbed down. Plain. It uses the words people actually use, in sentences structured the way people actually talk. It does not reach for the impressive turn of phrase. It reaches for the true one.

Sounds like:

"It does what it says. Nothing weird."

"For people who just want it to work."

"We're not going to oversell this. It's good. You'll like it."

"Built for regular people who have regular needs and don't want to think about it too much."

Does not sound like:

"Premium artisanal quality."

"Engineered for peak performance."

"Join our exclusive community."

The Visual World

Honest. Functional. Accessible. Real people, real environments, real moments without glamorization. The Everyperson's visual world does not have a high production budget look because that look signals a distance from ordinary life that this archetype cannot afford. It looks like something real people made for other real people.

Brand Examples

IKEA. The Everyperson brand at global scale. The stores are designed like homes. The prices are designed for real budgets. The product names are unpronounceable, which turns out to be charming rather than off-putting. IKEA treats its customers as capable adults who can assemble their own furniture. That respect is Everyperson.

Target. Premium prices? No. Premium experience? Also no. Premium accessibility: yes. Target is the Everyperson brand that understood that ordinary people still want things to look good, and built an entire positioning around making that possible without pretense.

Costco. No marketing. No loyalty program with a name. No brand advertising to speak of. Just a warehouse full of things that are good value for money. The Everyperson brand stripped to its absolute core.

Claim This Archetype If...

Your brand was built for the mainstream, not for a niche. Your audience wants reliability and accessibility over prestige. Your company culture is genuinely humble and unpretentious. The relationship you have with your customers is peer-to-peer rather than expert-to-novice.

Red Flags

You are using Everyperson language to cover for a lack of brand differentiation. Your brand is ordinary because you have not done the work to be anything else, not because ordinariness is a considered choice. Your audience actually does want aspiration and you are underserving them.

Brand Voice Exercise

Strip your best piece of brand content of every adjective that signals prestige, expertise, or uniqueness. What is left? If what remains is honest and warm, that is your Everyperson voice. If what remains is nothing, you have some work to do.

Activation Dare

Find the most common, ordinary use case for your product, the one you probably do not talk about because it is not impressive enough, and build a piece of content entirely around it. Celebrate the ordinary. No spin, no glamorization. See who recognizes themselves in it.

THE SAGE

"Truth over trend. Clarity over chaos."

The Character

The Sage knows. Not in a performative or pretentious way. In the quiet, certain way of someone who has done the work, earned the understanding, and is now ready to share it clearly, without agenda.

The Sage brand's most valuable asset is trust. Specifically, the kind of trust that is earned through demonstrated expertise over time, through the consistent experience of the audience coming to the Sage with a question and leaving with an answer they can actually use. The Sage does not traffic in opinion dressed as fact. The Sage does not speculate as if it were certain. The Sage says what it knows and acknowledges what it does not.

In a world drowning in information, the Sage archetype may be the most urgently needed. There has never been more content. There has never been more noise. There has never been a greater need for a source that the audience can trust to cut through it and tell them what is actually true.

The Sage's relationship with its audience is mentor-student in the best sense. Not hierarchical. Not condescending. Illuminating. The Sage makes the audience more capable, more informed, more equipped to navigate the world they are operating in. And because of that, the audience comes back.

Four Defining Traits

Knowledgeable. The Sage has done the work. It has the expertise. That expertise is not performed. It is demonstrated through the quality of what the Sage shares.

Objective. The Sage prioritizes truth over comfort. It will tell the audience something they do not want to hear if that is what the evidence shows.

Clear. The Sage can take complex things and make them navigable. Not by oversimplifying. By finding the right level of abstraction and the right structure for understanding.

Patient. The Sage does not rush the audience to understanding. It meets them where they are and brings them along.

The Voice in Action

Sage copy is precise and substantive. Every word earns its place. The Sage voice does not perform intelligence. It demonstrates it by being genuinely useful.

It is not flashy. It does not need to be. The Sage voice is confident because it is right, not because it is louder or bolder than everything else.

Sounds like:

"Here's what the research actually shows."

"Let's separate the signal from the noise."

"The conventional wisdom on this is wrong. Here's why."

"We don't know everything. Here's what we do know."

Does not sound like:

"We're disrupting the industry with…"

"Our proprietary insights give you the edge."

"Thought leadership for forward-thinking professionals."

The Visual World

Clean. Structured. Information-forward. The Sage visual world respects the content. Typography that prioritizes readability. Data visualized with care.

White space used to aid comprehension. The Sage's visual world says: the substance is the point. We are not trying to distract you from it.

Brand Examples

Google. At its core, Google is the Sage brand: the oracle that knows the answer to any question you can formulate. The search box is the Sage archetype made into a product.

TED. Ideas worth spreading. The Sage archetype in its most explicit form. The entire brand is built around the proposition that knowledge, shared clearly and compellingly, can change the way people see the world.

The Economist. Trusted by people who want to understand the world, not just be informed about it. The Economist Sage brand is built on a century of demonstrated analytical excellence.

Mayo Clinic. In healthcare, the Sage is the institution that is trusted to know. Mayo Clinic's content marketing is among the best Sage brand execution in any category: genuinely useful medical information, clearly communicated, with no hidden agenda.

Claim This Archetype If...

Your brand has genuine expertise that your audience values and trusts. You are willing to say things that are true even when they are unpopular or go against conventional wisdom. Your audience's primary need is understanding, not entertainment or inspiration. You have the discipline to prioritize substance over style.

Red Flags

Your Sage positioning is not backed by genuine expertise. You use authoritative language for opinions, not knowledge. Your content is designed to signal intelligence rather than to be genuinely useful. You are afraid to say what is actually true if it might alienate part of your audience.

Brand Voice Exercise

Identify the single most common misconception in your industry or category. Write the clearest, most honest correction of that misconception you can. No hedging. No caveats beyond what the evidence requires. That piece is your Sage voice at its sharpest.

Activation Dare

Publish a piece of content that says something your industry does not want said. Not provocative for its own sake. True. The thing that experts in your field know but nobody says publicly because it is inconvenient. The Sage's job is to say it. Say it.

THE INNOCENT

"Keep it simple. Keep it good."

The Character

The Innocent is not naive. The Innocent has looked at a complicated, noisy, often cynical world and made a deliberate choice: to respond to it with clarity, goodness, and the insistence that things can be exactly as good as advertised.

This takes more courage than it looks like from the outside. The Innocent brand resists the temptation to be clever, to be ironic, to add layers of sophistication that signal awareness of how difficult and complicated everything is. The Innocent says: we know. We have looked at all of it. And we still believe in this simple, good thing.

The Innocent's audience is not naive either. They are often people who have tried complicated solutions and are exhausted by them. People who want something that works, that is honest about what it is, that does not require translation or context or the decoding of marketing language. The Innocent brand is a relief.

The Innocent archetype requires the most internal alignment of any in the system. Because the Innocent's promise is fundamental goodness, any gap between that promise and the reality of how the company operates, how it treats its employees, how it sources its materials, how it handles a crisis, is immediately visible and deeply damaging. The Innocent must be good, not just appear to be.

Four Defining Traits

Optimistic. The Innocent genuinely believes things can be good. Not because it is ignorant of the challenges, but because it chooses to act from possibility rather than from fear.

Honest. The Innocent does not spin, does not obscure, does not use language to make things seem different than they are. The clarity is the brand.

Pure. In the sense of un-corrupted. The Innocent brand has not been compromised by the shortcuts, the cost-cutting decisions, the "good enough" thinking that erodes quality over time.

Simple. The Innocent finds clarity where others find complexity. It strips away what is unnecessary and holds onto what is true.

The Voice in Action

Innocent copy is clean and warm. Short sentences. Common words. No jargon. No irony. The Innocent voice sounds like a person talking to another person, directly, without performance.

It is not bland. Bland is the failure mode of brands that mistake simplicity for emptiness. The Innocent voice has warmth, sincerity, and a quiet confidence in the value of what it is offering.

Sounds like:

"It's just good fruit. That's it."

"We make this as well as we possibly can. We hope you taste the difference."

"No tricks. No fine print. Just this."

"Good things made honestly."

Does not sound like:

"Revolutionizing the way you think about..."

"Disrupting the category with our proprietary..."

"The world's most innovative approach to..."

The Visual World

Clean. Bright. Natural. Color palettes borrowed from the natural world: greens, whites, warm yellows. Photography that is sunny and unmanipulated. Typography that is simple and friendly. The Innocent visual world says: nothing here is trying to trick you. What you see is what you get.

Brand Examples

Innocent Drinks. The brand that essentially defined the Innocent archetype in consumer goods. From the handwritten font on the first bottles to the "little tastes of goodness" copy to the Innocent Foundation, every element of the brand is the archetype made visible.

Aveeno. Oat-based skincare that works. The Innocent brand in the beauty space: no miracle claims, no complex ingredient lists presented as science, just natural ingredients that are good for your skin.

Warby Parker. Started with a simple premise: glasses should not cost as much as an iPhone. The Innocent brand in retail: honest pricing, clear purpose, and a genuine desire to make a good product accessible.

TOMS. The "One for One" model is Innocent brand execution: a simple, clear, uncomplicated way to make buying something feel genuinely good. The brand does not ask you to understand a complex impact thesis. It just says: you buy these, a child gets a pair. That's it.

Claim This Archetype If...

Your product is genuinely simple and genuinely good. Your founding premise was to do something in a more honest, uncomplicated way than it was being done. Your audience is exhausted by complexity and looking for something they can trust. Your organization's values are genuinely aligned with the goodness you project externally.

Red Flags

Your Innocent positioning is a marketing choice, not an organizational reality. Your supply chain, your labor practices, or your business model has complexity that contradicts the innocent image. You are using simplicity as a substitute for substance. Your brand is Innocent in presentation but your audience's actual needs are complex.

Brand Voice Exercise

Take your most complicated piece of content and rewrite it using only words a twelve-year-old would know. Not because the content is for twelve-year-olds. Because the discipline of plain language reveals whether the complexity was necessary or defensive. What survives that rewrite is your Innocent voice.

Activation Dare

Publish something about your product with no marketing language at all. No adjectives that signal quality. No comparisons. No features. Just an honest description of what it is, who made it, and why. The equivalent of a handwritten label on a jar of jam. See who it reaches.

BRINGING IT ALL TOGETHER

You have now met all 12.

One of them should feel like home. Not perfect, not without tension, not without the red flags you will have to manage. But home.

If you are still uncertain between two or three, that is normal. Go back to the Field Assessment questions from Chapter 2. Look at the red flags for your top candidates. Ask honestly: which of these am I avoiding because I do not want to do the work the archetype requires?

That answer is usually the right one.

If you are certain, do not second-guess the certainty. Clarity is rare. Hold it.

The next step is the deep work: finding your voice inside the archetype you have claimed. That is Part Three. But before you go there, there is one more chapter in Part One that will make everything that follows more useful.

Chapter 4 bridges the archetype to the story. Because knowing who you are is only the beginning. The next question is: how do you tell the world?

Brand Deck Connection: All 12 Archetype Cards.

Pull the card for your primary archetype. Read the front and back. The card contains the condensed version of everything in this chapter for your archetype. Use it as a quick reference. Use this chapter as the depth behind it.

Next: Part Two. Tell Your Story.

Chapter 4: Why Story Is the Last Unfair Advantage.

CHAPTER 4:
Why Story Is the Last Unfair Advantage

"There is no greater agony than bearing an untold story inside you."

-- Maya Angelou

THE TEXTBOOK VERSION

The marketing process has five steps.

Step 1: Understand the marketplace and customers.

Step 2: Design a customer-driven marketing strategy.

Step 3: Construct an integrated marketing program that delivers superior value.

Step 4: Build profitable relationships and create customer delight.

Step 5: Capture value from customers to create profits and customer equity.

Execute all five correctly. Build the machine. Measure everything. Win.

THE FIELD VERSION

Notice what is not on that list.

Step Zero. The one that comes before understanding, before strategy, before delivering value, before any of it. The question every forgettable brand skips because it is not on the list and it does not fit neatly in a process:

Who is this brand? And what is the story only we can tell?

Process without identity is a treadmill. You can run it perfectly and never go anywhere. You can execute all five steps at a professional level and still produce a brand that lands like a press release in a world already drowning in them.

The missing step is not a tactic. It is not a content calendar or a narrative framework or a well-placed origin story on the About page.

It is the understanding that story is not a tool you use. Story is the thing your brand either is or is not. And if it is not, nothing in the five-step process will make up for that.

The Unfair Advantage Nobody Can Copy

Your competitor can match your price.

They can clone your product feature within eighteen months, maybe six. They can replicate your distribution channel. They can reverse-engineer your SEO. They can hire your VP of Marketing and find out exactly what you are doing.

They cannot copy your story.

Not your real story. Not the story rooted in who you actually are, what you actually believe, and why you actually exist. That story is not a marketing asset. It is a birthright. It is the thing that was true before you had a logo or a tagline or a deck to send to prospects.

Your story is the one competitive advantage that is genuinely defensible. And most brands either do not know it or do not tell it.

This is not a metaphor or a motivational poster. This is a structural observation about how markets work. When products and prices converge, as they always do in mature categories, story is what separates the brands people choose from the brands people settle for.

Choose and settle. Different words. Entirely different relationships.

What Story Actually Does to the Brain

Here is the neuroscience, stripped of the jargon.

When you give someone a list of facts, two parts of their brain activate. The language processing areas. Information goes in. Information gets filed. Maybe.

When you give someone a story, their brain synchronizes with the storyteller's brain across every region involved in experiencing what is being described. If there is a chase scene, the motor cortex fires. If there is an emotional moment, the limbic system engages. If there is a smell described in detail, the olfactory cortex activates.

The brain doesn't differentiate cleanly between experiencing something and hearing a well-told story about it.

This is called neural coupling. The brain of the listener literally mirrors the brain of the narrator. You are not transmitting information when you tell a story. You are transmitting experience.

Now ask yourself: what do your customers remember from your last marketing email? From your website's homepage? From your sales deck?

Features and pricing are facts. They activate two brain regions. They are processed and usually forgotten within 72 hours.

Story activates seven regions. It creates memory through emotion, not repetition. It builds trust through narrative familiarity, not through a longer list of credentials.

This is not an argument for making things up. The most powerful stories in brand history are true. They are specific, human, and inconveniently honest. They are powerful precisely because they do not sound like marketing.

That is the bar. True. Specific. Human. Inconvenient in the best possible way.

The Mistake That Kills Most Brand Stories

There is one storytelling error that shows up everywhere, across every category, every company size, every budget level.

The brand casts itself as the hero.

Look at almost any brand's website. The homepage tells you how long they've been in business, how many customers they serve, how many awards they have won, and why their product or service is different and better and special.

The subject of every sentence is the brand.

This is the wrong story.

Your customer is the hero. They are the one with the challenge, the transformation they need to make, the version of themselves they are trying to reach. They are Rocky at the bottom of the stairs. They are Luke with no idea what they're supposed to do next. They are the operator trying to figure out how to run a restaurant in a world that will not stop changing.

Your brand is not the hero. Your brand is the guide.

The guide has a role in every great story. The guide appears at the moment the hero needs exactly what the guide has to offer. The guide does not take over the hero's journey. The guide equips the hero to complete it.

Yoda does not fight Vader. Yoda trains Luke.

Gandalf does not carry the ring. Gandalf shows Frodo the way.

The Oracle does not free Neo. She tells him what he needs to hear to free himself.

This is the reframe that changes everything. The moment you stop writing about what your brand can do and start writing about what your customer can become, the story starts to work.

Try it on your own homepage. Change the subject of every sentence from "we" to "you." Watch what happens.

Story Works in Every Direction

Here is what most brand strategy advice misses about storytelling.

Story is not a channel.

You do not decide to "do storytelling" for Q3 and then return to normal marketing in Q4. Story is the operating layer underneath everything your brand does, everything your brand says, and everything your brand means to the people who choose it.

Story shows up in:

The one-line pitch. When someone asks what you do and you have ten seconds, story determines whether they lean in or zone out. "We help restaurants find labor-saving tech" is a fact. "We help operators stop losing sleep over who's going to show up on Saturday" is the beginning of a story.

The email subject line. A subject line is an open loop. It creates tension. It creates curiosity. The brain wants to close the loop. That is narrative mechanics at work in 60 characters.

The sales conversation. Your best salespeople are telling stories, not reciting value propositions. They are making the customer the hero of a before-and-after. They are naming the villain (the problem, the friction, the cost of inaction) before they ever introduce the product.

The customer testimonial. Every great testimonial is a mini Hero's Journey. There was a problem. Then there was a solution. Then there was transformation. The brands that understand this structure their case studies accordingly.

The onboarding experience. The moment a customer signs a contract or downloads your app, the story continues. The brands that design onboarding as a narrative arc see dramatically higher activation than the ones that treat it as a feature checklist.

The hire. The way you describe what working at your company actually means is a story. The brands that attract the right people tell a story worth working for. Not benefits and perks. A mission with stakes.

Story is not one thing you do. It is the connective tissue between every thing you do.

Why Some Stories Die Before They're Told

You have a story worth telling. Everyone does. The question is what gets in the way.

Problem one: Committees.

Brand stories told by committee end up sounding like exactly that. Every strong instinct gets softened. Every provocative phrase gets qualified. Every specific detail gets replaced with something broader so it doesn't exclude anyone.

What comes out the other end is beige. Safe. Forgettable.

The best brand stories are written by one voice, shaped by a clear archetype, and then trained across the team. Not designed by a vote.

Problem two: Fear of the specific.

Founders especially are afraid to make their story too specific. What if we say it's for restaurant operators and alienate the hospitality consultants? What if we commit to the challenger brand narrative and lose the enterprise prospects?

Here is what happens when you are specific: the right people recognize themselves. Here is what happens when you are vague: nobody does.

The most specific brands are the ones with the most loyal audiences. They chose a lane. The right people followed.

Problem three: Waiting for permission.

The story doesn't need to be perfect before you tell it. It doesn't need a brand agency to bless it. It doesn't need a style guide and a messaging matrix and six months of research before it can go into the world.

The story needs to be true. It needs to be specific. It needs to reflect who you actually are.

Everything else is polish. And polish can happen after the story is alive.

The Three Stories Every Brand Needs

Most brands try to tell one story and use it everywhere. This is better than having no story. But it doesn't give you the range you need to move people at different stages of the relationship.

There are three stories that matter.

The Origin Story. Why does this brand exist? Not the company founding story with dates and office locations and funding rounds. The human story. The problem that wouldn't let you go. The moment you realized the thing that existed wasn't good enough. The reason this needed to be built.

Origin stories do a specific job: they build trust with people who don't know you yet. They say, before you ask me to trust you with your business, let me tell you what we actually believe. This is where Rebel and Explorer archetypes especially shine. The origin is where they first showed up.

The Customer Story. A before-and-after told through a real person. Not a case study formatted like a business document. A narrative. Name the hero. Name the challenge. Show the transformation. Make it feel like something that could happen to the reader.

Customer stories do a specific job: they bridge the gap between curiosity and commitment. Prospects don't fully believe what you say about yourself. They do believe what someone like them says about their experience.

The Future Story. Where is this going? What does the world look like if what you're building works? What transformation are you part of creating?

Future stories do a specific job: they recruit. They attract the right employees, the right partners, the right investors, and the right early customers who want to be part of something that matters. A future story is a flag planted in the ground. The right people will walk toward it.

You need all three. They work at different ranges. They serve different audiences. Together they build a narrative world that people can enter from any direction and find their way in.

Scaffolding, Not Formula

The next chapter gives you 12 storytelling frameworks.

Before you get there, a word about what frameworks are and are not.

A framework is scaffolding. It gives your story a structure that has proven to work: a sequence, a tension, a resolution. It does not replace your story. It shapes it. The same way a sonnet is not the poem. The sonnet form is the structure. The poem is what you put inside it.

None of the 12 frameworks will work if you pour a generic, uncommitted, committee-approved brand narrative into them. They need your specific story, your actual conviction, your real archetype underneath.

With those in place, a framework makes a good story great. It adds momentum, tension, and resolution. It makes your truth easier to follow and harder to forget.

Without those in place, a framework is just a template. It produces something that looks like a story from a distance and sounds like nobody in particular up close.

The framework is not the unfair advantage. Your story is.

The framework is just how you tell it well.

Brand Deck Connection: Summary Card 2, Storytelling Frameworks.

This card is the at-a-glance guide to all 12 frameworks, including when to use each, which archetypes pair best, and the single best prompt to unlock the story your brand needs to tell. Pull it before you write anything. Then come back to Chapter 5.

Next: Chapter 5. The 12 Storytelling Frameworks.

Structure that lets your truth breathe.

CHAPTER 5:
The 12 Storytelling Frameworks

"A story with a shape is a story that sticks."

Twelve frameworks.

Each one has a structure. Each one has a job. Each one has been proven across thousands of brands, campaigns, origin stories, and sales conversations.

For every framework, you get: the structure, the job it does, the archetypes it fits best, a real-world brand example, messaging prompts you can use immediately, and an activation challenge to make it real.

Read them all. Even the ones that seem wrong for you. Especially those.

Then go to Chapter 6 to match your archetype to the frameworks that are built for you.

FRAMEWORK 1: The Hero's Journey

"It's dangerous to go alone. Take this."

The Structure

A hero lives in an ordinary world. Something disrupts it. A call to adventure arrives, and the hero hesitates. Then they cross the threshold into unfamiliar territory. They face trials, enemies, temptations, and the darkest moment. They find within themselves what they need. They win. They transform. They return home changed, carrying something of value for the people they left behind.

This is the oldest story in the world. It works because it is the shape of how human beings actually change.

The Job

Brand origin stories. Customer success stories. Product launches. Campaign narratives. Any time your brand is accompanying someone through a transformation, this is your structure.

Crucial reframe: Your customer is the hero. Your brand is the guide. The guide shows up with exactly what the hero needs at exactly the right moment. That is the role. Play it well.

Best Archetype Pairs

Hero, Explorer, Magician, Caregiver.

The Hero archetype guiding another hero is a natural fit. The Explorer draws the map the hero needs. The Magician hands over the thing that makes the impossible possible. The Caregiver is the steady companion through the trial.

Brand Example: Duolingo

The user is a person who always wanted to speak another language and never managed to. Ordinary world: monolingual, a little embarrassed, maybe a little defeated. Call to adventure: a new job, a trip, a relationship, or just the lingering feeling that this is the year. Threshold: first lesson. Trials: missed days, difficult vocabulary, the app's inexhaustible cartoon owl. Transformation: real, functional fluency and the identity shift that comes with it.

Duolingo never positions itself as the hero. It is the guide. The owl is the guide. The streaks are the stakes. You are the one doing the journey.

Messaging Prompts

- "What does your customer's ordinary world look like before they find you?"
- "What is the specific moment of disruption? The inciting incident?"
- "What is the deepest point of struggle? What does transformation look like on the other side?"

- "How does your brand play the guide? What specific thing do you hand them?"

Activation Challenge

Write your customer's Hero's Journey in six sentences. One sentence per stage: ordinary world, call to adventure, threshold, trials, darkest moment, transformation. Your brand appears in exactly one of those sentences. If it appears in more than one, revise.

FRAMEWORK 2: Problem-Agitate-Solve

"Twist the knife. Then offer the cure."

The Structure

Name the problem. Make the problem feel urgent and real and viscerally uncomfortable. Then offer the solution.

Three beats. Deceptively simple. One of the highest-converting structures in existence.

The Job

Sales pages. Email subject lines. Opening lines for any piece of content. Paid ads. Anything where you need to quickly earn the reader's attention by making them feel that you understand their actual situation.

The problem does the work of recognition. The agitate does the work of urgency. The solve does the work of relief.

Best Archetype Pairs

Hero, Rebel, Jester, Ruler.

The Hero makes the problem a challenge worth overcoming. The Rebel names the problem as a systemic injustice worth fighting. The Jester makes the problem darkly funny, which makes the solution feel like deliverance.

The Ruler names the problem as a matter of unacceptable disorder, then restores order.

Brand Example: Calendly

Problem: Scheduling a meeting requires an embarrassing number of emails where two professionals pretend to have no idea what "Tuesday around 2pm" means and both secretly resent every round trip.

Agitate: This is happening dozens of times per week. It is eating time you do not have. It is making you look less competent than you are. It is a solved problem that the world is still treating as unsolvable.

Solve: Calendly. One link. They pick the time. Done.

No features listed. No capability matrix. Problem, twist, relief. It reads in four seconds and converts in six.

Messaging Prompts

- "What is the specific, named pain your customer is living with right now?"
- "What does it cost them? Time, money, credibility, sleep, their sanity?"
- "How does your solution feel, not just what does it do?"

Activation Challenge

Write a PAS sequence in 75 words or less. Problem in one sentence. Agitate in two or three. Solve in one. If your solve sentence includes the words "innovative," "best-in-class," or "seamless," go back and write it in plain English.

FRAMEWORK 3: Before-After-Bridge

"Show the pain. Show the dream. Show the way."

The Structure

Before: the world the customer is living in right now. After: the world they want to be in. Bridge: your brand is the way to get from one to the other.

Contrast is the engine. The gap between Before and After is what creates desire. The Bridge is only as compelling as the gap it crosses.

The Job

Homepage headlines. Social ads. Email openers. Sales collateral. Any time you want to create aspiration and position your brand as the means to get there.

Best Archetype Pairs

Magician, Caregiver, Creator, Innocent.

The Magician transforms before into after and makes the bridge feel inevitable. The Caregiver holds the reader's hand across the gap. The Creator builds the thing that makes after possible. The Innocent promises a simpler, cleaner version of the after state.

Brand Example: Headspace

Before: stressed, distracted, running on fumes, convinced there is no time to slow down and also feeling the consequences of that every single day.

After: calmer, clearer, more present, sleeping better, less reactive. The version of you that handles things instead of enduring them.

Bridge: ten minutes. One session. Just start.

Headspace doesn't sell meditation. It sells the gap between who you are exhausted and who you could be calm. The bridge is almost offensively simple, which is exactly the point.

Messaging Prompts

- "Describe the Before state with enough specificity that your customer nods while reading it."
- "Describe the After state as a feeling, not a feature. What is different about their day, their business, their life?"

- "What is the single clearest version of the bridge? The simplest path from one to the other?"

Activation Challenge

Go to your homepage right now. Find your headline. Identify which of the three states it occupies: Before, After, or Bridge. If it occupies none of them, which is likely, rewrite it using this structure in under 12 words.

FRAMEWORK 4: Open Loop Narrative

"Start a story they have to finish."

The Structure

Open with a story that creates irresistible tension. Name a character, establish a situation, raise the stakes. Then withhold the resolution. Force the audience to keep reading, watching, or listening to close the loop.

The brain has a documented compulsion to complete unfinished narratives. This is called the Zeigarnik Effect. Use it.

The Job

Content marketing. Email opens. Video hooks. Podcast intros. Anything where the challenge is getting people to continue. The open loop makes stopping feel uncomfortable and continuing feel necessary.

Best Archetype Pairs

Rebel, Jester, Magician, Explorer.

The Rebel opens a loop that feels transgressive and urgent. The Jester opens a loop that is absurd and impossible to resist. The Magician opens a loop that feels mysterious and slightly impossible. The Explorer opens a loop that goes somewhere no one has been before.

Brand Example: Liquid Death

Liquid Death launched with a video called "Murder Your Thirst." The loop opened with the words: "Our biggest concern as a company is making sure that you don't die of boredom while you're drinking water."

This is a sentence that should not work. It is a water company claiming that water, historically the least interesting beverage in existence, is now a matter of life, death, and edge. The loop is open. The tension is: are they serious? What is this? I need to understand what is happening here.

You watch. You find out. You either love it immediately or you are deeply confused. Both responses are fine. The loop made you stay.

Messaging Prompts

- "What is the most unexpected or counterintuitive thing about your brand or category?"
- "What is a story from your company's history that raises a question before it gives an answer?"
- "What does your audience assume about your category that you can disrupt in one sentence?"

Activation Challenge

Write a three-sentence opener for a piece of content that ends with a question, an unresolved situation, or a provocative claim. Do not resolve it. Stop. That is the open loop. Your only job is making someone desperate to read sentence four.

FRAMEWORK 5: The Pixar Pitch

"Once upon a brand..."

The Structure

Six sentences. Each one building on the last, creating momentum toward a resolution that feels earned.

Once upon a time...

Every day...

Until one day...

Because of that...

Because of that...

Until finally...

That is the complete structure. Deceptively simple. Absolutely devastating in the right hands.

The Job

Brand origin stories. About pages. Investor narratives. Team all-hands. Any time you need to create emotional momentum in a short amount of time. This is the fastest path from "who are you" to "I get it, I'm in."

Best Archetype Pairs

Creator, Caregiver, Innocent, Everyperson.

The Creator's origin story is usually a Pixar Pitch waiting to be told. The Caregiver's reason for existing is almost always this shape. The Innocent's "things should just be good" conviction fits this structure perfectly. The Everyperson's "we're just like you" story finds its best form here.

Brand Example: Slack

Once upon a time, a company was building a video game and needed a way to communicate internally without drowning in email.

Every day, they sent messages to each other through a clunky internal system that frustrated them but was better than nothing.

Until one day, the game failed. The company pivoted. But the internal communication tool they had built for themselves was quietly excellent.

Because of that, they decided to build it properly and share it with the world.

Because of that, it spread through teams and companies almost entirely by word of mouth, team by team, department by department.

Until finally, it became the workplace communication platform used by millions of teams who all started it for the same reason: because someone in the office was tired of drowning in email and thought there had to be a better way.

Every team member who adopted Slack saw themselves in the origin. That is the structural genius of the Pixar Pitch: it gives the audience a way in.

Messaging Prompts

- "What was the ordinary world before your company existed?"
- "What was the disruption? What was the thing that made the old way untenable?"
- "What were the cascading consequences that led to where you are now?"

Activation Challenge

Write your brand's Pixar Pitch. Exactly six sentences. No sentence over 20 words. Do not add a seventh sentence. The discipline is the point.

FRAMEWORK 6: Villain-Solution-Victory

"Every great story needs a monster."

The Structure

Name the villain: the problem, the status quo, the way things have always been done that is making life worse for your customer. Give them the weapon: your solution, your approach, your product. Celebrate the victory: what becomes possible when the villain is defeated.

Great stories need conflict. Most brand stories are terrified of conflict. This framework leans in.

The Job

Category creation. Positioning against the status quo. Challenger brand narratives. Any time your brand exists because the old way was genuinely not good enough and someone needed to say it out loud.

Best Archetype Pairs

Rebel, Hero, Magician, Ruler.

The Rebel names the villain with relish and means every word. The Hero defeats the villain through will and effort. The Magician defeats the villain through transformation. The Ruler defeats the villain through superior order and standards.

Brand Example: Mailchimp

The villain: the old marketing software that was expensive, complicated, required an IT team to operate, and was clearly built for companies that weren't yours.

The solution: email marketing that a small business owner could actually use. No enterprise contract. No professional services required. Just you, your list, and a platform smart enough to help.

The victory: the small business owner who used to pay someone else to handle email marketing, or worse, just not do it, now does it themselves on a Tuesday afternoon, gets results, and feels like a legitimate marketer for the first time.

The villain is never Constant Contact or HubSpot. The villain is the complexity and gatekeeping that kept email marketing out of reach. Naming that villain clearly is what made Mailchimp feel like liberation, not just a cheaper alternative.

Messaging Prompts

- "What is the villain your customer is living with before they find you? Name it precisely."
- "What does the villain cost them? Be specific."

- "What does the world look like after the villain is gone? What is the victory?"

Activation Challenge

Name the villain in your category in one sentence. Do not name a competitor. Name the condition, the friction, the failure of the status quo. If it does not make your target customer say "yes, exactly," write it again until it does.

FRAMEWORK 7: The Brand Origin Story

"Why did this have to exist?"

The Structure

There are only three ingredients in a good brand origin story: a person, a problem they couldn't leave alone, and the moment they decided to do something about it.

That is it. No elaborate timeline. No board meeting. No Series A announcement. A person, a problem, and the moment of decision.

The Job

About pages. Founder social posts. Sales conversations where someone asks how you got started. Podcast appearances. Media pitches. The origin story is the most human version of your brand's reasoning and it is the only brand story that is completely uncopied.

No one can tell your origin story. Which means no one can compete with it.

Best Archetype Pairs

Every archetype. Every single one.

But they each tell the origin differently. The Rebel tells it as a reckoning: I looked at the way things were and I refused. The Explorer tells it as a discovery: I went looking for something and found something more important. The Creator tells it as an inevitability: I needed to build this thing or it would never exist. The Caregiver tells it as a calling: someone needed help and I was in a position to give it.

Your archetype shapes how your origin is told, even when the facts are the same.

Brand Example: Popcorn GTM

The problem was a category full of restaurant tech brands that all sounded the same. They all claimed to reduce costs and drive efficiency and support operators with best-in-class solutions. Nobody believed any of them, and the operators could not tell them apart.

The person was a marketer who had spent years watching great products fail to connect because the brands telling the story had no idea who they actually were or why it mattered.

The decision: stop working for companies that did not understand this and start working only with the ones willing to actually fix it.

That is the Popcorn GTM origin. Not a polished founding narrative. A reckoning and a refusal.

Messaging Prompts

- "What was the specific problem that made you feel like something needed to change?"
- "What was the moment you decided to stop accepting the problem and start solving it?"
- "What did you believe then that most people in your category still do not believe now?"

Activation Challenge

Write your origin story in 150 words. Person, problem, moment of decision. No company history. No credentials. No funding announcement. If it could be about any other founder in your category, it is not specific enough. Write it again.

FRAMEWORK 8: The Testimonial Remix

"Your customer already wrote the best copy."

The Structure

Take what your customers actually said, their words, their language, their specific description of the before and after, and give it structure. Layer in context. Name the hero. Make it a story, not a quote block.

The raw ingredients are already there. The Testimonial Remix is about recognizing them for what they are.

The Job

Case studies. Social proof. Sales enablement. Customer-led content. Email sequences. Any time you want the voice of the customer to do the convincing instead of your own.

The testimonial is the most trusted form of brand communication. Not because marketers say it is, but because people's bullshit detectors are calibrated to zero in on first-person, specific, human language. A testimonial written in plain English about a specific transformation is worth more than five polished brand claims.

Best Archetype Pairs

Caregiver, Everyperson, Hero, Creator.

The Caregiver's impact is almost always felt most clearly by the customer describing their experience. The Everyperson's relatability is validated most powerfully when a customer says "this is just like me." The Hero's transformation resonates when it is told by the person who lived it. The Creator's impact shows up in what the customer made possible with your tools.

Brand Example: Shifty

Shifty helps restaurant operators manage labor scheduling. Their testimonials don't read like quotes on a software review site. They read like this:

"I stopped coming in on Sundays to fix the schedule. I spent my first Sunday at home in three years. My kids thought I was sick."

That is not a testimonial. That is a Hero's Journey in three sentences. Ordinary world: working every Sunday. Transformation: first Sunday home. Resolution: so shocking to the family they thought something was wrong.

The brand did not write that. A customer did. The brand recognized what it was and put it where it could do the most work.

Messaging Prompts

- "What language do your best customers use when they describe what changed after working with you?"
- "What is the most specific, human, unexpected thing someone has said about the experience?"
- "What transformation do customers describe that you have been failing to communicate in your own copy?"

Activation Challenge

Pull the last ten pieces of customer feedback you received. Read them for story structure. Look for: a before state, a moment of change, an after state. Find the one that has all three and is the most specific. Structure it as a three-paragraph mini story. Headline: the transformation. Paragraph one: the before. Paragraph two: what changed. Paragraph three: the after, in the customer's own words.

FRAMEWORK 9: The Contrast Manifesto

"Not this. This."

The Structure

Define what you are against. Then define what you are for. Let the contrast do the positioning work.

This framework is a series of paired statements. Old world, new world. Wrong way, right way. What we refuse, what we believe. The opposition creates clarity. The clarity creates identity.

The Job

Brand manifestos. Website About sections. Social bios. Positioning documents. Any time you need to stake a claim and make it impossible to misread.

This is the framework for brands with genuine conviction about doing something differently. The ones who have something to push against. The ones who are tired of the category's safe defaults.

Best Archetype Pairs

Rebel, Explorer, Creator, Ruler.

The Rebel's manifesto is a declaration of what the establishment has gotten wrong and what freedom looks like instead. The Explorer's manifesto is what the old map missed and what happens when you go off it. The Creator's manifesto is what craft demands and what shortcuts cost. The Ruler's manifesto is what standards actually mean and what mediocrity actually does.

Brand Example: BrewDog

BrewDog's original Equity for Punks manifesto was a Contrast Manifesto at full volume.

We are not a regular beer company.

We don't believe in the way beer has always been made, marketed, and sold.

We believe in craft. In ingredients that mean something. In people who give a damn.

Not corporate. Not compromised. Not beige.

The contrast is the positioning. You know exactly who they are because you know exactly what they are not.

Messaging Prompts

- "What does your category do by default that you refuse to do?"
- "What do you believe that most of your competitors would be afraid to say out loud?"
- "If your brand were a person, what would be on their non-negotiable list?"

Activation Challenge

Write a Contrast Manifesto for your brand. Seven paired statements. Old world versus new world. Use "Not [X]. [Y]." as your sentence structure. The discipline is keeping both sides specific. Generic contrasts produce generic manifestos. Name the actual thing you're pushing against.

FRAMEWORK 10: The Prediction Story

"Here is what happens next. You can be ready or not."

The Structure

Identify a shift happening in your market, category, or customer's world. Name what it means. Position your brand as the guide through what's coming.

This is a thought leadership framework. It builds authority by demonstrating that your brand can see around corners.

The Job

Keynotes. Conference presentations. Trend reports. LinkedIn long-form posts. Podcast appearances. Any time your brand needs to establish authority before a sale, not during it.

The Prediction Story doesn't sell. It teaches. It earns trust by giving something valuable before asking for anything in return. That trust is what eventually converts.

Best Archetype Pairs

Sage, Magician, Explorer, Ruler.

The Sage predicts from data and earned wisdom. The Magician sees the transformation before it happens and shows others how to get ahead of it. The Explorer has been to where things are heading and is reporting back. The Ruler names the new standard before the market has agreed to it.

Brand Example: Patagonia

Patagonia has been making the same environmental prediction since before it was mainstream: the way we produce, consume, and discard is not sustainable, and the brands that choose to change now will be on the right side of what is coming.

This is a prediction story. It has been told since Yvon Chouinard was making gear in a tin shed. The prediction is still being borne out. The authority is enormous precisely because the prediction was unpopular when it was first made and correct when the world caught up.

Messaging Prompts

- "What is changing in your customer's world faster than they realize?"
- "What are the brands or leaders who ignore this shift going to look like in five years?"
- "What does your brand understand about this shift that positions you to guide people through it?"

Activation Challenge

Write a Prediction Story in 300 words. Name the shift. Describe what it means for the people you serve. Name one thing they can do right now to get ahead of it. Do not name your product. The prediction stands on its own. The credibility it builds will do the selling later.

FRAMEWORK 11: The Day in the Life

"Show, don't tell."

The Structure

Put the reader inside a specific day, a specific moment, a specific experience of your customer's life. Make it vivid enough that they recognize themselves. Then show what changes when your brand is in the picture.

This is immersive storytelling. It does not explain the value proposition. It makes the reader feel it.

The Job

Video scripts. Social content. Long-form content marketing. Product pages that need to do more than list features. Any time the gap between "I understand what this does" and "I feel what this would mean for me" is too wide.

Best Archetype Pairs

Lover, Caregiver, Everyperson, Creator.

The Lover makes the day-in-the-life sensory and rich. The Caregiver makes it warm and specific and human. The Everyperson makes it recognizable in a way that creates immediate identification. The Creator makes it about the process of making something, which is deeply satisfying to watch even before you are the one doing it.

Brand Example: Airbnb

Airbnb does not advertise hotel alternatives. It shows you a morning in a Lisbon apartment, a specific neighborhood, a specific window with specific light. You can smell the coffee. You can imagine what it sounds like at 7am when the market is setting up below.

The product is a booking platform. The story is a specific day in a specific life that you have not lived yet but immediately want.

Messaging Prompts

- "Describe your customer's morning before they had your product. Be specific."
- "Describe their morning after. What is different? What do they notice?"
- "What is the single sensory detail that makes the transformation feel real and not abstract?"

Activation Challenge

Write a Day in the Life sequence. Two paragraphs. Paragraph one: the before, in the morning, before your brand. Paragraph two: the same morning after. Use second-person voice: "you." Keep both paragraphs under 100 words. Make it specific enough that a real customer would say "that is exactly my life."

FRAMEWORK 12: The Values Story

"What we believe, demonstrated."

The Structure

Tell a story about a decision your brand made that revealed what you actually stand for. Not the stated values on the wall. The values that showed up under pressure, when it cost something to hold them.

Values demonstrated through action are the most powerful form of brand proof. Stated values are words. Demonstrated values are evidence.

The Job

Crisis communications. Brand culture content. Reputation building. Any time your brand needs to show who it is instead of saying it.

This framework is particularly important for brands at a moment of trust-building, either entering a new market, recovering from a misstep, or establishing credibility in a category where trust is the purchase trigger.

Best Archetype Pairs

Caregiver, Innocent, Ruler, Hero.

The Caregiver's values show up when they choose the customer's wellbeing over their own convenience. The Innocent's values show up when they hold their standards even when cutting corners would have been easier and no one would have known. The Ruler's values show up when they hold the standard even for the smallest thing because standards are not situational. The Hero's values show up when they show up, at the moment when showing up cost them something.

Brand Example: Patagonia (again)

When Patagonia received a $10 million tax windfall in 2017, they donated the entire amount to environmental groups. No announcement strategy. No marketing campaign built around it. They did it and then said they did it.

That is a Values Story. The action came first. The story followed. The story worked because the action was real and specific and cost something.

Messaging Prompts

- "When did your brand face a choice between the easy thing and the right thing, and choose the right thing?"
- "What does your brand refuse to do even when doing it would be profitable?"
- "What decision made internally, a hire, a policy, a product change, reveals who you actually are?"

Activation Challenge

Write a 200-word Values Story. Name a specific decision your company made, in the last two years if possible, that revealed something true about what you stand for. No hypotheticals. No abstractions. A specific event, a specific choice, a specific result. Share it somewhere public within 30 days.

Choosing Your Framework

Twelve frameworks. One brand. Where do you start?

Start with the job.

What does this piece of content, this campaign, this launch need to accomplish? Get someone's attention for the first time? Build trust with someone who already knows you? Move someone who is curious to committed? Close the gap between "this seems interesting" and "I'm in"?

Each framework has a job. Match the job to the moment.

Then go to Chapter 6, which matches framework to archetype. Not all frameworks work equally well for all archetypes. The ones that fit yours will feel natural. The ones that don't fit will feel like wearing someone else's clothes.

Know the job. Know your archetype. Pick the framework that sits at the intersection.

Then write something real.

Brand Deck Connection: Summary Card 2, Storytelling Frameworks.

The card lists all 12 frameworks with their core structure in one sentence each. Use it as a quick-reference before any content project. It also includes the single best prompt for unlocking your brand's primary story: "What problem would still exist if your brand disappeared tomorrow?"

Next: Chapter 6. Match Your Archetype to Your Framework.

Not every story structure fits every identity. Here's the map.

CHAPTER 6:
Match Your Archetype to Your Framework

"Know who you are. Then choose the structure that lets who you are come through."

You now have two things.

You have your archetype. The identity at the core of your brand. The character you are at the bone.

You have 12 storytelling frameworks. Proven structures that create momentum, tension, and resolution. Each one built to do a specific job.

Now you need to connect them.

Because not every framework fits every archetype. A Caregiver running a Villain-Solution-Victory story feels off-key. A Ruler doing a Day in the Life needs to be in the right hands or it reads like a brochure. A Jester attempting a straight Hero's Journey needs a twist built in or the whole thing collapses under the weight of sincerity.

Get the pairing right and the story flows. The archetype gives the framework its voice. The framework gives the archetype its shape. Together they produce something that feels inevitable, not assembled.

This chapter is the map.

How to Use This Chapter

Every archetype gets a profile with three elements:

Primary Frameworks: The structures this archetype was built for. These are natural fits. Put your archetype inside these frameworks and the story almost writes itself.

Secondary Frameworks: These work with some calibration. They are not the default, but in the right campaign, for the right moment, they can be powerful.

What to Watch Out For: The structural traps that specific archetypes fall into, and how to avoid them.

After the archetype profiles, there is a pairing matrix at the end for quick reference.

THE FREEDOM FAMILY

The Rebel, The Explorer, The Magician

These archetypes push boundaries, go places others haven't, and transform what they touch. Their stories tend to lean into disruption, discovery, and the gap between what is and what could be.

THE REBEL

Primary Frameworks

Villain-Solution-Victory. This is the Rebel's home turf. The Rebel exists because something is wrong. The establishment is broken. The industry is corrupt. The status quo is harming people who deserve better. The villain is not a competitor. The villain is the system, the old way, the comfortable lie everyone has agreed to accept. Name it. Take it apart. Show what happens when it falls.

Contrast Manifesto. The Rebel's worldview is built on refusal and replacement. Not this. This. The manifesto is where the Rebel gets to draw the line in public and invite people to stand on the right side of it. BrewDog. Harley-Davidson. Oatly. These brands built their following by standing for something by standing against something else first.

Open Loop Narrative. The Rebel excels at creating tension. They know how to start a story that doesn't feel like it should exist, that makes people lean in because they cannot figure out where it is going. Open it with a provocation. Withhold the resolution. Watch the algorithm reward the discomfort.

Secondary Frameworks

Brand Origin Story, Prediction Story.

The Origin works when the founding story is itself an act of rebellion. The Prediction works when the Rebel is predicting the collapse of the thing they're fighting, not just describing it.

What to Watch Out For

Rebellion without a point. The Rebel's power comes from the fact that the fight is real, the villain is real, and the cost is real. Rebel energy deployed purely for aesthetic, edgy for edgy's sake, rings hollow fast. The audience can tell the difference between a brand that means it and a brand that decided rebellious was a good look.

Also: the Rebel does not always win. Some of the most powerful Rebel stories end in productive failure, in burning the thing down so something better can grow. Don't sand off the edges with a forced triumphant resolution.

THE EXPLORER

Primary Frameworks

The Hero's Journey. The Explorer was built for this structure. Their customer is always crossing a threshold, leaving something familiar for something unknown. The Explorer is the guide who has already been there. The frameworks fits the archetype like a map fits a landscape.

Prediction Story. The Explorer has already been to where things are heading. They report back. They tell you what they found around the next bend before the rest of the market knows the bend exists. This is the Explorer's thought leadership play and it is exceptionally powerful because it is credible. They went. They looked. They know.

Open Loop Narrative. The Explorer's curiosity is contagious. They start stories the way they start journeys: by pointing at something on the horizon and refusing to look away until they understand what it is. The open loop suits this perfectly.

Secondary Frameworks

Day in the Life, Brand Origin Story.

Day in the Life works when the Explorer's world is vivid and specific enough to make the reader want to be in it. The Origin works when the founding story is a literal departure: a moment when the founder left the known world behind.

What to Watch Out For

The Explorer's biggest trap is wandering without returning. Every great journey ends with a return, with the traveler coming back changed and carrying something worth sharing. Explorer brands that only point outward, always seeking, never arriving, never delivering the insight, leave their audience feeling restless rather than inspired. Land the plane. Tell them what you found.

Also watch the romance of difficulty for its own sake. Exploration is compelling. Endless exploration as a brand identity starts to feel like avoidance.

THE MAGICIAN

Primary Frameworks

Before-After-Bridge. The Magician's fundamental move is transformation. Before the Magician, ordinary. After, extraordinary. The Before-After-Bridge is the structural home of transformational brands. Use it to show the gap between what is and what becomes possible. The bridge is your brand's magic.

Pixar Pitch. The Magician's story is almost always a story about an unexpected transformation: something changed, cascading consequences followed, and the world is different now. The Pixar Pitch's "because of that, because of that" structure captures the momentum of transformation better than any other framework.

Day in the Life. The Magician makes the extraordinary feel tangible. The Day in the Life, written through the Magician's lens, shows the after state in such sensory detail that the transformation feels real and accessible, not theoretical.

Secondary Frameworks

Villain-Solution-Victory, Prediction Story.

The villain for the Magician is the small, limited, uninspired version of what something could be. The victory is the full expression of the possible. The Prediction works when the Magician is forecasting a shift that most people haven't felt yet but will.

What to Watch Out For

Vagueness. The Magician's language tends toward the transcendent, words like transform, elevate, reimagine, unlock. These words are not wrong. They are just empty until you fill them with specific, concrete proof. Apple talks about transformation but they show you exactly what it looks like in a specific product doing a specific thing. Nail the specificity or the magic disappears.

Also: the promise and the proof need to match. The Magician can make a very large promise. That promise needs to be delivered. The brand that overpromises and underdelivers does not feel magical. It feels like a trick.

THE SOCIAL FAMILY

The Hero, The Lover, The Jester

These archetypes are built around emotion, energy, and human connection. Their stories tend to be kinetic, felt, and impossible to ignore.

THE HERO

Primary Frameworks

Hero's Journey. Yes, obviously. But here is the nuance: the Hero archetype playing the Guide role in the Hero's Journey produces some of the greatest brand stories ever told. Nike does not tell the story of Nike. Nike tells the story of the athlete who will not stop, who gets up earlier, who pushes further. Nike is the guide. The athlete, the customer, is the hero. That inversion is what made Nike culturally massive.

Villain-Solution-Victory. The Hero's other home. The Hero exists to overcome. The villain is the obstacle, the resistance, the challenge, the inner voice that says you cannot do this. Name the villain. Give the customer the means to defeat it. Celebrate the victory that proves they always had it in them.

Problem-Agitate-Solve. The Hero brand can name the problem with moral clarity. This is what you're up against. This is what it's costing you. Here is what you do about it. The Hero's urgency makes the agitate hit hard without feeling manipulative.

Secondary Frameworks

Testimonial Remix, Values Story.

The Testimonial Remix for a Hero brand is a victory story told by the person who lived it. The Values Story shows the Hero brand showing up when it mattered, the moment of demonstrated commitment that proves the brand means what it says.

What to Watch Out For

The Hero archetype must be careful not to be the hero of its own story. This is the mistake that turns powerful Hero brands into chest-thumping brands. The customer is always the hero. Your job is to hand them the sword, train them, believe in them when they doubt themselves, and then step back.

Also: Hero brands can tip into relentless intensity that leaves no room for humanity. Even Gatorade has ads that smile.

THE LOVER

Primary Frameworks

Day in the Life. The Lover lives in sensation, detail, and felt experience. The Day in the Life framework, written through the Lover's lens, is a fully immersive experience. It shows you exactly what it smells like, feels like, sounds like to be in the Lover brand's world. Chanel doesn't tell you about a fragrance. It puts you inside the moment the fragrance was made for.

Before-After-Bridge. The Lover's transformation is emotional and sensory, not just functional. Before: ordinary, unfeeling, going through the motions. After: alive, present, moved. The bridge is the experience the Lover brand creates. This framework lets the Lover show the gap between existing and living.

Brand Origin Story. Lover brands almost always have a founder who was moved by something, who made something because they felt it, not because they identified a market opportunity. That origin story, told in the Lover's specific, sensory, personal voice, is irresistible.

Secondary Frameworks

Open Loop Narrative, Testimonial Remix.

The Lover's open loop is desire, tension before release. The Testimonial Remix for a Lover brand is an emotional before-and-after, the person who describes not what the product did but what they felt.

What to Watch Out For

Sentimentality. The Lover's emotional register is high. High emotion done well is powerful. High emotion done carelessly tips into saccharine, overwrought, or worse, manipulative. The antidote is specificity. Specific details earn emotion. Vague emotion requests it without earning it.

Also: the Lover brand needs to know who it's speaking to. Intimacy requires proximity. You cannot be intimate with everyone. The Lover's voice needs a specific person on the receiving end or it dissipates.

THE JESTER

Primary Frameworks

Open Loop Narrative. The Jester's open loop is absurdist and irresistible. They open with something that doesn't make sense in the best possible way, and the audience stays because they have to know where this is going. Liquid Death. Old Spice. Aviation Gin. The hook is always a little wrong in a way that makes it feel completely right.

Contrast Manifesto. The Jester's manifesto is funny. The contrast is between the industry's pomposity and the Jester's refusal to participate in it. The "Not this. This." structure, in the Jester's hands, becomes comedic and true at the same time. Both things make it memorable.

Problem-Agitate-Solve. The Jester's PAS makes the problem darkly comic, which is deeply effective. When you laugh at something it becomes real in a way that straightforward description cannot achieve. The agitate hits harder when it makes you laugh first. Then the solve lands as both relief and punchline.

Secondary Frameworks

Testimonial Remix, Hero's Journey.

The Jester's Testimonial Remix mines customer reviews for unintentional comedy and structural brilliance. The Hero's Journey, with the Jester as guide, is absurdist and delightful: the unlikely mentor, the ridiculous trials, the victory that makes no sense and perfect sense simultaneously.

What to Watch Out For

The Jester's biggest threat is the brand that thinks it's funnier than it is. Jester energy requires actual wit. Forced humor is the worst possible outcome. If the joke needs explaining, it is not a Jester brand. It is a brand that wishes it were.

Also: the Jester can tip into irrelevance. Being funny is not sufficient. The humor has to be in service of something: a truth, a tension, a genuine connection with the audience. Comedy is not a strategy. Comedy is how this archetype delivers its strategy.

THE ORDER FAMILY

The Caregiver, The Creator, The Ruler

These archetypes build, protect, and structure. Their stories tend to be grounded, earned, and sustained by demonstration rather than declaration.

THE CAREGIVER

Primary Frameworks

Hero's Journey. The Caregiver is the natural guide archetype. Their customer is always facing something difficult. The Caregiver's job is to equip, steady, accompany. The Hero's Journey framework with the Caregiver as the guide is one of the warmest and most effective brand narratives available.

Testimonial Remix. No archetype benefits more from the customer's own voice than the Caregiver. Because the Caregiver's value is felt, not analyzed, the testimonial is the proof. The customer who describes the moment your brand showed up for them is doing the work no copywriter can do.

Values Story. The Caregiver's values show up in action. The moment they chose the harder right over the easier wrong. The policy that costs more but protects better. The decision that puts the customer's wellbeing ahead of the brand's convenience. Write those stories.

Secondary Frameworks

Before-After-Bridge, Pixar Pitch.

The Before-After-Bridge for the Caregiver is a relief story: from stress, fear, or uncertainty to safety, clarity, and support. The Pixar Pitch for the Caregiver is often the founder's empathy origin, the moment they felt the thing their customer was feeling and decided to do something about it.

What to Watch Out For

Martyrdom. The Caregiver can drift into a sacrificial narrative that makes the brand feel heavy rather than comforting. People want to feel cared for, not guilty about being cared for.

Also: the Caregiver that over-promises safety or emotional outcomes they cannot guarantee damages trust in a way that is very hard to recover from. The Caregiver's credibility is entirely built on follow-through. Promise what you can deliver. Deliver more than you promised.

THE CREATOR

Primary Frameworks

Brand Origin Story. The Creator's origin is almost always a compulsion: the thing they had to make because it didn't exist yet. That origin story, told specifically and honestly, is the most powerful piece of content a Creator brand has. It is the story that attracts the right employees, partners, and early customers, the people who are also compelled.

Pixar Pitch. The Creator's founding narrative follows the Pixar Pitch structure almost inevitably. The gap in the world that needed filling. The cascading "because of that" moments. The thing that was built because it had to be. The Pixar Pitch gives the Creator's passion a shape that others can follow.

Day in the Life. The Creator's Day in the Life is about the process of making. Watching someone create something, the iteration, the frustration, the breakthrough, is deeply compelling. Adobe and LEGO both understand this. The creative process is the story.

Secondary Frameworks

Contrast Manifesto, Values Story.

The Creator's manifesto is about craft versus compromise, about the real thing versus the shortcut. The Values Story shows the Creator holding the standard in a moment where letting it slip would have been easy and no one would have known.

What to Watch Out For

Navel-gazing. The Creator loves the work. But the audience cares about what the work does for them, what it allows them to make, build, or express. Keep the camera on the customer's creative output, not just the brand's.

Also: Creator brands can become precious. The language of craft, done wrong, becomes gatekeeping. The best Creator brands make creativity feel accessible, not exclusive.

THE RULER

Primary Frameworks

Villain-Solution-Victory. The Ruler's villain is disorder, mediocrity, the tolerance of standards that shouldn't be tolerated. The victory is order, quality, and the feeling of being in the right hands. American Express, Mercedes-Benz, and IBM all run this story. The villain is not a competitor. The villain is the unacceptable alternative.

Prediction Story. The Ruler's thought leadership play is to set the standard before the market has caught up. To predict not just where things are heading but what the new expectation should be. The Ruler's prediction is a statement of future requirements disguised as a forecast.

Contrast Manifesto. The Ruler's manifesto is a declaration of standards. This is what excellence looks like. This is what we will not accept. The contrast is between what could be and what mediocrity produces.

Secondary Frameworks

Values Story, Testimonial Remix.

The Values Story for the Ruler is the moment the standard was held when no one would have noticed if it slipped. The Testimonial Remix captures the relief of being in expert hands, the customer who describes the feeling of having someone else handle something important correctly.

What to Watch Out For

Distance. The Ruler's authority can create a coldness that alienates the very people they're trying to attract. Authority without warmth is intimidation, not leadership. The best Ruler brands are authoritative and assured, not aloof.

Also: the Ruler cannot afford to be wrong publicly. The authority is built on demonstrated competence and credibility. A Ruler brand caught in a quality failure, a recall, a service disaster, loses something that is very expensive to rebuild.

THE BELONGING FAMILY

The Everyperson, The Sage, The Innocent

These archetypes build trust through familiarity, wisdom, and simplicity. Their stories tend to be honest, grounded, and easy to believe because they never promise more than they can deliver.

THE EVERYPERSON

Primary Frameworks

Testimonial Remix. The Everyperson's most powerful voice is the customer's own voice. The brand speaks for the people because the people recognize themselves in the brand. The testimonial is not a marketing tactic for this archetype. It is the primary mode of communication.

Day in the Life. The Everyperson's Day in the Life is recognizable in the most powerful way. The reader sees their own morning, their own kitchen, their own commute. They feel seen. That feeling of recognition is the Everyperson's core value proposition and the Day in the Life delivers it better than any other structure.

Before-After-Bridge. The Everyperson's bridge is not dramatic or transcendent. It is practical and real. The before is genuinely uncomfortable and relatable. The after is better in modest, achievable, believable ways. IKEA does not promise an extraordinary life. It promises a better living room. That restraint is the power.

Secondary Frameworks

Pixar Pitch, Problem-Agitate-Solve.

The Pixar Pitch for the Everyperson is a founding story about someone just like the customer who had the same problem and decided to build the solution. The PAS, in the Everyperson's hands, is relatable rather than urgent. The problem is familiar. The solve is accessible.

What to Watch Out For

Blandness. The Everyperson's commitment to relatability can flatten into having no personality at all. The goal is to be recognizable to your audience, not to be invisible to everyone. You still need a point of view. You still need something worth saying. Being approachable is not the same as being forgettable.

Also: condescension. The Everyperson brand that talks down to the people it claims to represent destroys trust instantly and completely.

THE SAGE

Primary Frameworks

Prediction Story. The Sage has earned the right to say what is coming. Their authority is built on demonstrated knowledge and track record. The Prediction Story is the Sage's highest-leverage format because it does the most important thing a Sage can do: give the audience something genuinely useful before they've asked for it.

Problem-Agitate-Solve. The Sage's PAS is educational and clear. The problem is named with precision. The agitate comes from clarity, not urgency: this is what happens when the problem goes unaddressed. The solve is delivered with evidence and confidence. No hype. Just the right answer, demonstrated.

Hero's Journey. The Sage is the archetypal guide. They appear at the moment the hero needs exactly what the Sage has. They give the hero what they need to see clearly, to act correctly, to complete the journey. The Sage as guide in the Hero's Journey is one of the most credible brand roles available.

Secondary Frameworks

Contrast Manifesto, Values Story.

The Sage's manifesto is about truth versus misinformation, clarity versus complexity, the real answer versus the convenient one. The Values Story shows the Sage telling the inconvenient truth when the convenient lie would have been easier.

What to Watch Out For

Condescension. Knowledge without empathy is lecturing. The Sage's authority is earned and shared, not wielded. The moment the Sage starts making the audience feel stupid, the relationship ends.

Also: the Sage must be right. The authority is entirely built on the quality of the information and the track record of being correct. A Sage brand caught spreading misinformation, even accidentally, loses the one thing they have. Accuracy is not optional. It is the brand.

THE INNOCENT

Primary Frameworks

Before-After-Bridge. The Innocent's bridge is from complicated, cynical, or compromised to simple, good, and clean. The before is the world's noise. The after is the quiet that happens when things are just what they say they are. The bridge is the Innocent brand's product or experience.

Pixar Pitch. The Innocent's founding story is usually a refusal: someone who looked at the category and decided that what was there was too complicated, too artificial, too compromised, and built the simpler, cleaner thing instead. That refusal, structured as a Pixar Pitch, is the perfect Innocent origin.

Values Story. The Innocent holds its standards not because someone is watching but because the standard is the point. The Values Story, for an Innocent brand, is the moment they chose the more expensive natural ingredient, the cleaner process, the higher standard when the shortcut was available and the customer would never have known.

Secondary Frameworks

Testimonial Remix, Day in the Life.

The Innocent's testimonials are simple and specific: "it just works," "I finally trust what I'm putting in my body," "it does exactly what it says." The Day in the Life is uncomplicated and warm, a morning that is simply better because the right thing showed up in it.

What to Watch Out For

Naivety. The Innocent's optimism is genuine and compelling. But a brand that pretends the world's complexity doesn't exist loses credibility with the people who know better, and everyone knows better eventually. The Innocent can hold its values without pretending the challenges don't exist.

Also: the Innocent cannot afford a scandal. The entire brand is built on the promise of purity, authenticity, and following through. A values violation is not a PR crisis for an Innocent brand. It is an identity crisis. The prevention is the only real strategy.

Building Your Core Story Stack

Here is how to apply this map in practice.

Step 1: Identify your primary archetype.

If you have not done this yet, go back to Chapter 2. Your primary archetype is the non-negotiable. Everything in your story stack needs to be consistent with who you are at the core.

Step 2: Find your primary framework.

Look at your archetype's primary frameworks. Which one fits the story your brand most needs to tell right now? Not every story, every campaign, every piece of content. The core story. The one that is most true and most urgent.

Step 3: Pick one secondary framework for a specific channel or moment.

Different frameworks work at different stages of the customer relationship. An open loop narrative earns attention. A Hero's Journey builds connection. A testimonial remix closes belief gaps. Map your secondary framework to the specific job you need it to do.

Step 4: Test for voice consistency.

Write one paragraph using your chosen framework. Read it out loud. Does it sound like your archetype? Does it sound like a specific person with a specific point of view? Or does it sound like it could belong to any brand?

If you can swap logos and it still works, you haven't found your voice yet. Go back to Chapter 7.

One More Thing

The frameworks are tools. The archetype is the hand holding them.

The same framework, run through two different archetypes, produces two completely different stories. A Hero's Journey told by a Jester is irreverent, self-aware, and probably features an absurd mentor. A Hero's Journey told by a Caregiver is warm, steady, and the guide shows up without being asked. Same structure. Entirely different stories.

This is why archetype comes first. Always.

Know who you are. Choose the structure that lets who you are come through. Write the story that only your brand can tell.

That is the whole game.

Next: Part Three. Find Your Voice.

Chapter 7: Voice Is the Fingerprint.

What your archetype sounds like when it opens its mouth.

CHAPTER 7:
Voice Is the Fingerprint

"Style is knowing who you are, what you want to say, and not giving a damn."

-- Gore Vidal

THE TEXTBOOK VERSION

The marketing concept holds that firms achieve their goals by satisfying the needs and wants of consumers better than the competition. The evolution of marketing philosophy ends here: customer-centric. Find out what they want. Give it to them better than anyone else. This is the final, highest form of marketing thinking. Customer first. Always.

THE FIELD VERSION

Customer-centric is right. As far as it goes.

But there is a step the textbook skips. A step that comes before customer-centric can mean anything at all.

Before you can be centered on your customer, you have to be centered on yourself. You have to know who this brand is. Not as a positioning exercise. Not as a statement in a brand guide that lives in a folder no one opens. As an actual, embodied identity with a specific way of seeing the world and a specific way of expressing that view.

Customer-centric thinking without an archetype foundation produces brands designed by consensus. Voice that sounds like it was written by a committee that polled everyone and committed to no one. Copy that could belong to any competitor in the category because it belongs, in truth, to none of them.

Research can tell you what your customer wants.

It cannot tell you who you are.

That is not a research question. That is a soul question. And this chapter is where you answer it.

What Voice Actually Is

Ask most marketers what brand voice is and they will show you an adjective list.

Bold. Authentic. Approachable. Human. Innovative.

These are not a voice. These are aspirations. Every brand in existence would claim most of these words. They say nothing about how a brand actually sounds in a sentence, a subject line, a social post, a sales email, a response to a negative review at 9pm on a Thursday.

Voice is not adjectives. Voice is choices.

The specific words you choose instead of the generic ones. The sentence length you favor. The rhythm of how you build an argument. What you refuse to say. How you handle disagreement. Whether you use humor and what kind. How formal or informal you go in a given context. The specific references you make. The things you would never say, not because they're wrong, but because they're not you.

Voice is the accumulation of thousands of choices, made consistently, over time, until the pattern becomes unmistakable.

You know a good brand voice the same way you know a good writer. You could read an uncredited piece and know who wrote it. The voice is identifiable without the byline. That is the bar.

Voice Versus Tone

These two things are not the same. Confusing them is one of the most common and costly brand communication errors.

Voice is who your brand is. It is permanent. It does not change based on context, channel, audience, or campaign. A Hero brand's voice is driven, direct, and challenge-oriented in January and also in December. In a LinkedIn post and also in a product cancellation email. Under pressure and when things are going well.

Voice is constitutional. It reflects the archetype at the core. You do not adjust it. You refine it, develop it, and express it with increasing precision over time, but you do not swap it out.

Tone is how you calibrate your voice for a specific moment. Tone is variable. It is appropriate to shift. A Caregiver brand whose voice is warm and supportive can have a different tone in a patient-facing clinical guide than in a recruitment post than in a founder's keynote than in a response to a crisis. The tone shifts. The underlying voice does not.

The error most brands make is treating voice as if it were tone: adjusting it to fit the room. The result is a brand that sounds different every time you encounter it, inconsistent, untrustworthy, and ultimately forgettable.

Think about how this works with a real person. A person has a character. They are curious or irreverent or precise or warm. That character shows up whether they're at a job interview, at a dinner party, or talking to a child. They calibrate. They don't transform. The person at the job interview is still recognizably the same person you'd want to grab a beer with.

Your brand is the same person everywhere it shows up. Different rooms. Same character.

The Cost of No Voice

You need to understand what sameness actually costs before you will commit to fixing it.

Open five competitor websites in your category right now. Read the homepage headline of each one. The About page. The first paragraph of a blog post.

How many of them use the word "innovative"? How many use "seamless"? How many promise to "empower" someone to do something? How many describe themselves as "passionate" about their industry?

How many of them sound like the same brand?

This is the commodity trap at the language level. When every brand in a category sounds alike, none of them have a voice. What they have is a genre. Marketing copy genre. Slightly corporate, vaguely optimistic, aggressively non-specific.

The customer reads all of them and feels nothing. They make their decision on price, or on a referral from someone they trust, or on which brand they happened to encounter first. Not on meaning. Not on connection. Not on the feeling that this brand gets them in a way the others don't.

Voice is what creates that feeling. And that feeling is worth money. Real, measurable, compounding money. Not as a soft metric. As a revenue driver.

Brands with a distinct voice command higher prices because distinctiveness signals value. They retain customers longer because the connection is emotional, not just transactional. They get shared more because there is something recognizable worth sharing.

The cost of no voice is a brand that competes on price and feature parity in a race that no one wins.

Voice Drift

There is another enemy. Slower than no voice and harder to see coming.

Voice drift.

A brand finds its voice. It is good. Sharp, specific, recognizable, and right for who they are. Then six months pass. Someone new joins the team and writes a different way. An agency produces a campaign in a different register. The CEO rewrites the homepage because they wanted it to sound more "professional." The investor deck gets a different tone than the website. The customer emails get outsourced.

Nobody makes a single decision to abandon the voice. A hundred small decisions slowly hollow it out.

Two years later the brand sounds like a different company. The customers who loved the original voice notice something is off but cannot name it. The new audience never gets to experience what made the brand special because that version no longer exists.

Voice drift is endemic. It happens to almost every brand that doesn't protect against it actively. The protection is not a style guide in a folder. It is a shared understanding, across every person who writes for your brand, of who this brand is and what it sounds like. An understanding specific enough that they can apply it without asking for permission.

That shared understanding starts with the archetype. It gets built in Chapter 8. And it only works if it is treated as a living, enforced standard, not a one-time deliverable.

Your Archetype Is Your Foundation

Everything about voice flows from archetype.

The Rebel does not sound like the Innocent. The Sage does not sound like the Jester. The Lover does not sound like the Ruler. Not because one is better or worse, but because they are different characters with different convictions and different ways of engaging with the world.

Your archetype tells you:

What you say. The topics you go deep on, the arguments you make, the questions you ask, the things you refuse to be neutral about. A Rebel brand has opinions about what's broken. A Sage brand has opinions about what's true. A Creator brand has opinions about what excellence looks like and what compromise costs.

How you say it. Sentence length. Vocabulary range. Whether you use humor and what kind. How direct you are. Whether you explain your reasoning or just make the call and move on. Whether you use data or stories or both. How you handle contradiction and challenge.

What you don't say. The words, phrases, and tones that are definitionally off-brand. The Jester does not write like a government document. The Innocent does not use cynical humor. The Ruler does not grovel. The Everyperson does not use jargon designed to make the reader feel less than.

The relationship you create. Are you a peer, a teacher, a guide, a companion, a challenger? Your archetype defines the nature of the relationship. The voice is how you show up in that relationship, every time.

The work in Chapter 8 is to take your archetype and translate it into a working voice system. Tools you can actually use. Standards specific enough to write from, not just aspire to.

What a Real Voice Sounds Like

Three quick examples of brand voices that are genuinely unmistakable. You know who they are before you see the logo.

"The things you own end up owning you."

You do not need the word Fight Club on that sentence. You know exactly where it's from. The Rebel voice at full volume: provocative, anti-accumulation, more interested in freedom than comfort. Three sentences into a piece of Tyler Durden's dialogue and you know the character completely.

"Just do it."

Not just a tagline. A voice. The Hero voice compressed to its irreducible core. Command tense. No qualifications. No explanation of why or how. The assumption is that you already know the challenge and you just need someone to refuse to let you make excuses. The entire Nike voice is in those three words.

"Think different."

Grammatically debatable. Strategically perfect. The Magician voice: slightly rule-breaking, confident, and aimed at the person who already suspects they see the world differently than everyone else and wants a brand that confirms it. Two words. Entire archetype.

These brands do not have adjective lists that say "bold, authentic, empowering." They have a voice that is those things, proved through the choices they make every time they write a sentence.

That is the goal.

Voice as a Competitive Asset

One last thing before we build yours.

Voice is a moat.

Product features get copied in months. Pricing strategy gets matched in weeks. Channel strategy gets cloned in days. Nobody can copy your voice. Not because it's legally protected, though it's yours, but because voice is emergent. It comes from the actual identity of the actual people behind the brand. You cannot fake it at scale. You cannot reverse-engineer it from the outside. You can imitate someone's vocabulary and sentence structure but the voice itself, the felt sense of who this is and what they believe, only comes from the real thing.

The brands with the most durable market positions are almost always the brands with the most distinct voices. They are recognizable regardless of format or channel or campaign. You know them before you see their name.

That is what you are building.

Not a document. Not a style guide. An identity expressed so clearly and consistently in language that it becomes part of how the market understands you.

And the market cannot take that away.

Brand Deck Connection: Summary Card 3, Voice and Tone.

This card is the orientation point for all eight Voice + Tone tools in Chapter 8. It also includes the Voice Rinse Test and the single question that tells you immediately whether your brand has a voice or just has words: "If you removed the logo, would anyone know it's you?"

Next: Chapter 8. The Voice Toolkit.

Eight tools for building a voice your whole team can actually use.

CHAPTER 8:
The Voice Toolkit

"A tool is only as good as the hand holding it. But first you need the tool."

Eight tools.

Each one is a practical exercise, not a conceptual framework. Each one produces something real you can use: a document, a list, a test, a constraint. Together they build a voice system that any writer, designer, marketer, or AI prompt can work from.

You do not need all eight today. Start with the ones that feel most urgent. But over time, work through every one. Each tool illuminates something different about your voice, and the combination is what makes the system durable.

TOOL 1: The Tone Spectrum

"Your voice isn't one-note, but it's not all over the place either."

What It Is

A map of where your brand lives on four axes. Not where you want to live. Where you actually live, today, based on what your brand sounds like in practice.

The Four Axes

Formal .... Informal

Bold .... Reserved

Warm .... Cool

Playful .... Serious

These are not binary choices. They are spectrums. Every brand sits somewhere on each line.

How to Use It

For each axis, place your brand. Not where you think it should be. Where your actual existing content would place it if you read it honestly. The homepage. The last email campaign. The most recent social post. The sales deck intro.

Then answer these questions:

- Is this where we want to be? If not, where is the gap?
- Does our placement vary wildly between channels? If yes, why?
- Is there an axis where we're being inauthentic, performing a version of ourselves that doesn't match our archetype?

The Output

A tone position for your brand. Four axes, four placements. This becomes the reference when someone asks "how formal should this be?" or "can we use humor here?" The answer is not a judgment call. It is the map.

The Calibration Rule

Your placement on the spectrum does not change between channels. But how far you push toward either end does. A Jester brand is always on the playful end. On LinkedIn they are playful and considered. On Instagram they are playful and quick. On a customer service email they are playful and warm. Same end of the spectrum. Different volume.

Activation

Map your brand across all four axes right now. Do it twice: once for how you want to be perceived, once for what your actual content suggests. Find the gaps. Those gaps are the brief for your next voice work.

TOOL 2: How We Speak / How We Don't

"Define your edges, or someone else will."

What It Is

Two columns. A contrast list. The simplest, fastest, and most durable voice tool available.

Column one: how this brand speaks. Column two: how this brand definitively does not.

Why It Works

Most brand voice guides tell writers what to do. They list the attributes, the adjectives, the aspirational descriptors. This tells writers what to avoid. And what to avoid is often clearer and more actionable than what to do.

"Write boldly" is a fuzzy instruction. "Never hedge with 'we think' or 'it seems'" is specific. "Be warm" is aspirational. "Never use corporate jargon like 'leverage' or 'synergize'" is a real rule.

The Don't column does the heavy lifting.

How to Use It

Build both columns in a session with your best brand writer or your founding team. Generate 10-15 items on each side. Then test them against your existing content. Find the places where the Don'ts are already showing up. Those are your voice leaks. Fix them.

Sample for a Rebel/Explorer Brand

HOW WE SPEAK:

- Direct. We say the thing.
- Short sentences when making a point. Longer when building an argument.
- Specific. Concrete nouns. Actual numbers when they matter.
- First person, second person. We and you.

- Earned confidence. We don't prove we're right. We demonstrate it.
- References that are alive: culture, sport, food, the real world.
- Humor that makes a point. Comedy in service of truth.

HOW WE DON'T:

- Corporate speak. Not ever. No "leverage," "best-in-class," "synergy," "utilize."
- Passive voice. No "it was found that." Someone found something.
- Hedging. No "we think," "it seems," "perhaps." Say it or don't say it.
- Hollow claims. Not "innovative" without evidence of what specifically is innovative.
- Humble brag dressed as humility.
- Jargon as a substitute for explanation.
- Em dashes. At all. Ever.

The Output

A two-column reference document. Short enough to actually read. Specific enough to actually use. Post it where your writers can see it.

Activation

Do this exercise now. Spend 20 minutes. Column one: ten things your brand does say and how. Column two: ten things your brand never says and never does. Read the finished list out loud. If any item in either column could belong to your competitor without modification, make it more specific.

TOOL 3: Voice Ingredients

"Every voice has a recipe."

What It Is

Your brand voice broken into three to five defining attributes, with relative proportions assigned to each.

Not adjectives. Attributes. The difference: an adjective describes. An attribute defines a behavior.

Why Proportions Matter

Saying your brand is "bold, curious, and warm" tells a writer three things in equal weight. That produces a very different voice than 50% bold, 30% curious, and 20% warm. The proportions are the recipe. Same ingredients, different balance, different dish.

How to Build It

Start by identifying your three to five strongest voice attributes. These should be specific to your archetype and visible in your best existing content.

Some starter attributes by archetype family:

Freedom archetypes: Defiant, Provocative, Searching, Transformative, Irreverent

Social archetypes: Driven, Sensory, Playful, Galvanizing, Intimate

Order archetypes: Authoritative, Precise, Compassionate, Innovative, Standards-holding

Belonging archetypes: Accessible, Wise, Honest, Familiar, Optimistic

Choose yours. Then assign percentages that total 100. Be honest about where the weight actually lives, not where you wish it did.

Sample: Popcorn GTM

40% Direct (we say the thing, short sentences, no hedging)

30% Sharp (specific, referenced, earned, never vague)

20% Curious (we ask the uncomfortable question, we notice what others don't)

10% Warm (we give a damn about the humans in the work, we have a sense of humor)

Every piece of Popcorn content should feel like those proportions. A post that is 80% warm and 20% sharp is off-brand even if it is well-written.

The Output

A voice recipe. Three to five attributes with percentages. This becomes the rubric when you review content for voice. Not "does this feel right?" but "does this have the right proportion of each ingredient?"

Activation

Write your voice recipe. Then take three recent pieces of your content and score them against it. How well does each one reflect the proportions? Where is the content skewing off-recipe? That's the direction your next voice revision goes.

TOOL 4: Voice as a Character

"If your brand could walk into a room, who would it be?"

What It Is

Your brand personified as a specific character. Not a demographic, not an archetype, not a persona. A human being with habits, opinions, and a way of taking up space.

Why This Works Better Than Adjectives

When you brief a writer with adjectives, they produce adjective-shaped content. When you brief a writer with a character, they produce human content. The character gives them access to specificity that no style guide can provide.

The character is the shortcut.

How to Build It

Answer these questions about your brand as if it were a person:

- What do they do for work? What did they do before?
- What do they read, watch, listen to?
- How do they walk into a room? First to speak or last?
- What are they certain about? What are they still figuring out?
- What do they find genuinely funny?
- What makes them angry?
- What do they refuse to do?
- What are three things they would never say at dinner?
- Who do people think of when they meet them?

Sample: Popcorn GTM

The Popcorn GTM brand is the consultant who has been in the room when the deal fell apart and knows exactly why. They read Fast Company but they'd rather read McSweeney's. They find most marketing jargon genuinely offensive, not strategically, but aesthetically: it's imprecise, it's cowardly, and it wastes everyone's time.

They walk in with coffee, they sit at the end of the table, and they wait for the moment when everyone has said the safe thing before they say the true thing. Not to be difficult. Because someone has to.

They would never say "circle back." They would never tell you you're doing great when you're not. They have opinions about restaurant tech that most people in restaurant tech are afraid to say out loud.

Brief a writer with that character and they know exactly what to write and what not to write. No adjective list required.

The Output

A character brief. One to two paragraphs. Specific enough that two different writers would produce content that sounds like the same person.

Activation

Write your brand character in 150 words. Read it to someone who works with your brand. Ask them: does this sound like us? Does this sound like someone you'd want to listen to? Revise until both answers are yes.

TOOL 5: What We Never Say

"Kill the cringe before it kills your brand."

What It Is

The Nope List. A documented inventory of specific words, phrases, constructions, and tones that are definitionally off-brand.

This is not a content policy. This is a voice standard. The things on this list are not wrong. They are not you.

Why This Is as Important as What You Do Say

Voice is as much about refusal as expression. The Rebel's voice is defined partly by what it refuses. The Innocent's voice is defined partly by what it will not allow in. The Sage's voice is defined partly by the certainty that precision is not negotiable.

The Nope List is the guardrail. It is where you prevent voice drift from the outside in.

How to Build It

Start with the words your category defaults to that you find deadening. Add any phrases that sound like they were written by algorithm. Add the tones that feel wrong for your archetype. Add the things that, when you see them in your own copy, make you wince.

Categories to cover:

Words and phrases to ban: Leverage, synergy, seamless, innovative, robust, utilize, best-in-class, transformative (unless you can prove it), solutions, ecosystem, empower (as a filler word).

Constructions to avoid: Passive voice. Hedging with "we think" or "it seems." Opening sentences with "We're excited to announce." Sentences that start with "At [Brand Name], we believe..."

Tones to prohibit: Corporate formal where informal is earned. Humble brag dressed as vulnerability. Urgency manufactured for no reason. Filler optimism ("We're so grateful for this amazing community!").

Specific to your archetype:

- Rebel/Rebel: False modesty. Political neutrality on things that aren't actually neutral. Anything that sounds like it was approved by legal before it was approved by truth.
- Sage: Vague claims of expertise. "Many experts believe." Citations without specificity. Wisdom theater without the receipts.
- Caregiver: Cold efficiency language. Clinical detachment. Anything that sounds like a form letter.
- Jester: Forced sincerity. Explained jokes. Safe humor that offends no one and delights no one.

The Output

A specific, documented Nope List. Organized by category. Short enough to actually post somewhere. Updated when new cringe words enter the category vocabulary.

Activation

Audit your last five pieces of published content against this list. How many Nope List items appear? Circle each one. That is your next editing pass.

TOOL 6: The Voice Rinse Test

"If you swapped logos, would anyone notice?"

What It Is

The simplest diagnostic in brand voice. A single test that tells you immediately whether your content has a voice or just has words.

The Test

Take a paragraph of your brand's copy. Any paragraph. A homepage section, an email intro, a LinkedIn post, a product description.

Remove the brand name from the copy. Remove any product-specific references.

Now read what's left.

Ask: could this belong to a competitor? Could it belong to any brand in your category that describes itself as "innovative," "customer-centric," and "passionate about solving problems"?

If the answer is yes, the voice doesn't exist yet. You have content. You do not have a brand voice.

Why This Test Is Merciless and Necessary

Most brands believe they have a voice. Most brands are wrong. The belief usually comes from having a tone guide or a style document. The test is whether the output produced by that guide is actually distinguishable from the output produced by any other brand's guide.

The Voice Rinse Test removes the illusion. It shows you exactly what you have.

The Passing Standard

A piece of content passes the Voice Rinse Test when a person familiar with your brand can identify it without the logo. Not because of specific product references, because of the voice itself: the sentence rhythms, the specific vocabulary, the particular way of seeing the world, the unmistakable character.

Run this test quarterly on a sample of your best content. Run it immediately on anything you're unsure about before publishing.

Activation

Pick your homepage's About section. Remove all brand references. Send it to three people who know your brand well and three who don't. Ask both groups: whose brand does this sound like? If the people who know you can identify it and the strangers can feel the specificity of the voice, you pass. If everyone shrugs, go back to Tools 1-5.

TOOL 7: Voice DNA

"If you disappeared tomorrow, how would someone describe you?"

What It Is

The atomic-level breakdown of your brand's voice. The specific patterns that make your writing immediately recognizable even without a byline. Not the adjectives. The actual mechanics.

What Voice DNA Captures

Signature phrases: The specific expressions your brand uses repeatedly that become part of how people think about you. These emerge naturally in great brand writing. You can also build them intentionally.

Sentence rhythms: Do you favor short declarative sentences that hit like punctuation? Long, building arguments that earn their conclusions? Mixed rhythm that creates momentum through contrast? Rhythm is one of the most distinctive elements of voice and the hardest to fake.

Punctuation patterns: Do you use dashes, parentheses, ellipses? Do you avoid them? Do you fragment sentences for effect? Do you ask questions directly to the reader? These choices create a recognizable visual and rhythmic signature.

Word-level patterns: Vocabulary range. Whether you use contractions. How you handle numbers. Whether you use slang and what kind. Whether you use foreign words or technical terms, and if so, whether you explain them or assume knowledge.

Reader relationship markers: Do you address the reader directly? Do you use "we" or "I"? Do you ask the reader questions? Do you challenge them? These choices define the nature of the relationship the writing creates.

How to Extract Your Voice DNA

Pull your 10 best pieces of brand writing. The ones that, when published, felt most like you. Read them with a specific eye for pattern. What is consistent across all of them? What specific choices appear in most of them?

Document what you find. That is your Voice DNA.

The Output

A brief, specific voice pattern document. Not a list of adjectives. A list of actual writing behaviors. Specific enough that a writer could use it to reverse-engineer your voice.

Activation

Find the single best piece of content your brand has ever published. The one that, when you read it, you thought "yes, this is exactly us." Analyze it for DNA. List every specific choice you can identify: sentence length, vocabulary, structure, rhythm, reader relationship. Then use that list as the brief for the next piece.

TOOL 8: Voice Shifts by Channel

"Same brand. Different room."

What It Is

A channel-by-channel guide to how your voice calibrates without changing. Same character, different volume, different register, different speed.

The Core Principle

Your brand does not have a different voice on LinkedIn than on Instagram. It has the same voice in different rooms.

Think about the person you identified in Tool 4, your brand character. That person behaves differently at a conference keynote than at a dinner party than in a text message than in a formal proposal. Their character is consistent. Their calibration is not. They know the room.

Your brand needs to know the room too.

Channel Profiles

LinkedIn: Professional but not corporate. Your most considered content. The place for the Prediction Story, the thought leadership play, the 400-word observation that earns a response. Even Jester brands calibrate up on LinkedIn, not to stuffiness, but to "I have something worth your attention."

Instagram: Faster, more visual, more sensory. The rhythm is different. The caption is doing less work because the image is doing more. Creator, Lover, and Jester brands live here. Sage and Ruler brands can too if they know how to translate their authority into a visual language.

Email: The most intimate channel. The reader has given you their inbox. The voice here should feel personal, direct, and worth the open. Short paragraphs. One point per email. The subject line is a story hook, not a subject matter descriptor.

Website homepage: The first impression and the fastest judgment. You have eight seconds. Your voice needs to be unmistakable in that time. The archetype should be identifiable from the headline alone.

Sales conversations: The voice is the same but the conversational register is more adaptive. You are listening more. But your brand character still shows up in how you ask questions, what you care about, what you refuse to say.

Customer service: Where voice is tested most. The person writing the service email is often not the person who built the brand. The Caregiver's warmth, the Hero's directness, the Sage's clarity, these need to show up even when someone is unhappy. Especially when someone is unhappy.

How to Build Your Channel Guide

For each channel where your brand is active, answer three questions:

1. What is the reader's state of mind when they encounter us here?
2. How does our voice calibrate for that state of mind?

3. What specific adjustments do we make to length, register, and speed?

The Output

A one-page channel calibration guide. Each channel, two to three sentences of guidance. Not a full style guide per channel. A calibration note: "Here we go faster and shorter." "Here we earn the space." "Here we are at our most human."

Activation

Pick your three primary channels. For each one, write one paragraph of content in your brand voice, calibrated for that specific room. Read all three out loud. They should sound like the same person in three different conversations, not three different people.

Putting the Voice Toolkit Together

You do not need to run all eight tools in a single session. You need to run them systematically over time and update them as your brand evolves.

A suggested order for getting started:

4. **How We Speak / How We Don't** (Tool 2) first. This produces something usable immediately.
5. **Voice Ingredients** (Tool 3) next. This gives you the recipe to check everything against.
6. **Voice as a Character** (Tool 4) to give the recipe a face.
7. **The Nope List** (Tool 5) to build the guardrails.
8. **The Voice Rinse Test** (Tool 6) as an ongoing diagnostic.

Tools 1, 7, and 8 are refinement tools. Run them after you have the foundation. Use them to tune what you've built.

The full system, built and maintained, is what turns a brand voice from a creative idea into a company-wide standard. It is what lets every writer, in every channel, on every day, sound like the same brand.

That consistency is what makes the voice compound.

Brand Deck Connection: Summary Card 3, Voice and Tone.

Each of the eight tools in this chapter corresponds to a Brand Deck Voice + Tone card. Pull them for workshops, briefings, or when you need a fast reset on whether your content is on-voice. The cards are designed to work alone or together, in sequence or as individual diagnostics.

Next: Chapter 9. Writing in Your Archetype's Voice.

Theory meets the page. What each archetype sounds like when it writes a sentence.

CHAPTER 9:
Writing in Your Archetype's Voice

"The difference between the right word and the almost right word is the difference between lightning and a lightning bug."

-- Mark Twain

Here is a sentence.

Read it carefully.

"We are a leading provider of innovative solutions that help businesses achieve their goals and drive sustainable growth."

This sentence exists on thousands of websites right now. Possibly tens of thousands. It contains the words "leading," "innovative," "solutions," "goals," and "sustainable growth." It has a subject, a verb, and an object. It communicates nothing.

Not because it is badly written. It is technically fine. It has grammar and syntax and a recognizable structure.

It communicates nothing because it could belong to any brand, in any category, at any moment in history since 1994. It has no voice. It has no character. It reveals nothing about who wrote it or why they exist or what they actually believe.

This chapter takes that sentence and twelve others like it and runs them through all twelve archetypes.

Same information. Different character. Different world.

By the end you will know exactly what your archetype sounds like when it opens its mouth and exactly what it sounds like when it forgets who it is. Both are useful. The contrast is the lesson.

How to Use This Chapter

For each archetype you get:

The Voice Profile: What this archetype sounds like at the sentence level. The rhythm, the vocabulary, the relationship with the reader, the specific things that make it unmistakable.

The Rewrite: The generic corporate sentence transformed through this archetype's lens. Watch what changes. Watch what stays.

Sounds Like / Does Not Sound Like: Two short samples. One on-voice, one off. The contrast is the teaching.

The Most Common Mistake: The specific voice failure that each archetype is most prone to. Where the voice collapses, and why.

The Rewrite Challenge: A second piece of generic copy for you to try on your own.

THE FREEDOM FAMILY

THE REBEL

"Rules were made to be broken."

Voice Profile

The Rebel is declarative. It does not explain itself before making a claim. It makes the claim and trusts that the right people will follow. Sentences are short and sometimes deliberately blunt. The vocabulary leans toward the direct over the diplomatic. Humor is dark, dry, or cutting. The Rebel calls things what they are: broken, wrong, dishonest, a racket, a lie everyone has agreed to pretend is true.

The Rebel does not soften its edges to be more palatable. It accepts that some people will be put off. That is a feature, not a bug. The audience who responds to the Rebel is the audience who has been waiting for someone to say the real thing.

The Rewrite

Before: "We are a leading provider of innovative solutions that help businesses achieve their goals and drive sustainable growth."

After: "The industry told you this was complicated. It isn't. We built the thing that was supposed to exist already and somehow never did. You're welcome."

Sounds Like

"The old way is broken. We know it, you know it, and everyone pretending otherwise is selling something."

Does Not Sound Like

"We're passionate about disrupting conventional approaches to deliver game-changing value for our stakeholders."

(That is a Rebel costume on a Ruler body. The language of rebellion with none of the actual rebellion. The Rebel can smell it from across the room.)

The Most Common Mistake

Rebellion as aesthetic. The Rebel that uses edgy language without having anything real to push against sounds like a brand that read about punk rock and decided to wear the jacket without learning the chords. The fight needs to be real. The villain needs to be real. The cost of the old way needs to be specific and honest or the whole thing collapses into posturing.

Rewrite Challenge

Generic: "Our team of experienced professionals is committed to delivering exceptional customer service and building long-term relationships with our clients."

Your turn. Make it Rebel. Name what's broken. Say the true thing.

THE EXPLORER

"Go your own way."

Voice Profile

The Explorer's voice is curious and in motion. It leans forward. It asks questions not as a rhetorical device but because it actually wants to know the answer. The rhythm tends to be expansive, building, then landing on something specific discovered at the end of the thought. The vocabulary is alive to the physical world: terrain, direction, what's over the next ridge, what you find when you actually go look.

The Explorer resists certainty as a pose. It is comfortable with "I don't know yet, but here is what I found when I went looking." Authority is earned through having gone somewhere, not through credentials.

The Rewrite

Before: "We are a leading provider of innovative solutions that help businesses achieve their goals and drive sustainable growth."

After: "We got tired of the map everyone was using. Went off it. Found something better. Here's what we brought back."

Sounds Like

"Most brands never leave the marked trail. We keep going until the trail runs out. That's usually where the interesting stuff starts."

Does Not Sound Like

"We empower organizations to explore new frontiers of operational excellence and navigate the evolving landscape of modern business."

(This is Explorer vocabulary with no actual exploration in it. "Frontiers" and "navigate" are borrowed metaphors, not lived ones. The real Explorer's language comes from having actually gone somewhere.)

The Most Common Mistake

Wandering without arrival. The Explorer's curiosity is its greatest asset and its greatest vulnerability. Content that asks good questions, builds genuine momentum, then never lands anywhere useful leaves the reader stranded. Every expedition needs a return. Every discovery needs to be delivered. The most powerful Explorer content goes out, finds something real, and comes back with it.

Rewrite Challenge

Generic: "We leverage cutting-edge technology and industry best practices to provide scalable solutions for businesses of all sizes."

Make it Explorer. Go somewhere. Come back with something real.

THE MAGICIAN

"Turn insight into alchemy."

Voice Profile

The Magician's voice is visionary and exact at the same time. It sees something others don't see, and it describes what it sees with surprising precision. The rhythm tends to build from an ordinary observation to an extraordinary conclusion: the gap between what is and what could be is where the Magician lives. The vocabulary is elevated without being inaccessible. It uses the unexpected word, the reframe, the pivot that makes the reader see the same thing completely differently.

The Magician does not explain the trick. It shows the result and lets the wonder do the work.

The Rewrite

Before: "We are a leading provider of innovative solutions that help businesses achieve their goals and drive sustainable growth."

After: "You have a business. We see what it could become. The gap between those two things is exactly where we work."

Sounds Like

"The ordinary version of this already exists. We make the version that shouldn't be possible and then show you how to use it."

Does Not Sound Like

"We transform organizations through cutting-edge innovation and visionary leadership to unlock unprecedented potential."

(The Magician's words. The Magician's energy. None of the Magician's specificity. "Unprecedented potential" is a promise without a shape. The Magician always shows you what the transformation looks like, not just that transformation is available.)

The Most Common Mistake

Promising without proving. The Magician's voice can ascend so far into the possible that it loses contact with the demonstrable. Transformation is a big word. It needs to be earned with specific evidence: what changed, for whom, from what to what. The Magician who can only gesture at the miraculous without showing the before and after eventually loses the audience's willingness to believe.

Rewrite Challenge

Generic: "Our comprehensive platform enables organizations to streamline workflows, improve efficiency, and make data-driven decisions."

Show the transformation. Make it specific. No empty superlatives.

THE SOCIAL FAMILY

THE HERO

"Challenge accepted."

Voice Profile

The Hero's voice is direct, active, and built for motion. Passive voice does not exist here. Every sentence has a subject doing something. The rhythm is driven and intentional, building toward a clear point rather than circling it. The vocabulary is concrete and kinetic: push, build, earn, fight, show up, do the work. The Hero does not hedge and does not comfort. It challenges.

The relationship with the reader is one of earned respect. The Hero treats the reader as someone capable of more than they are currently doing, and the writing reflects that expectation.

The Rewrite

Before: "We are a leading provider of innovative solutions that help businesses achieve their goals and drive sustainable growth."

After: "Your competitors are not waiting. Neither should you. We build the tools that go to work when everyone else is still deciding."

Sounds Like

"This isn't for everyone. If you want easy, we're not it. If you want results, let's talk."

Does Not Sound Like

"We're here to support your journey and help you achieve your unique vision of success through our comprehensive suite of services."

(Support and journey and unique vision. This is the Hero archetype with the challenge removed. The Hero does not offer support. The Hero offers a dare. The Hero does not describe your vision to you. It shows you what you are capable of and makes you prove it.)

The Most Common Mistake

Making the brand the hero. The Hero archetype is the most prone to this error because the energy is so kinetic and confident that it naturally wants to be about the brand's strength. Resist it. The reader is the one who overcomes. The brand is the one who hands them what they need to do it. Every "we crush" should be a "you can."

Rewrite Challenge

Generic: "We are dedicated to helping our clients succeed through personalized support and customized solutions designed to meet their specific needs."

Give it the Hero's voice. Make it a dare, not a promise.

THE LOVER

"Feel something."

Voice Profile

The Lover's voice is sensory and unhurried. It earns the right to slow down. It uses specific, physical details that activate the senses: texture, light, smell, the particular quality of a moment. The rhythm is more lyrical than punchy, building feeling rather than making points. The vocabulary is rich without being overwrought. The Lover does not rush to the conclusion. The experience is the conclusion.

The relationship with the reader is intimate. The Lover writes like it knows who is reading, not a customer, a specific human being with desires worth understanding.

The Rewrite

Before: "We are a leading provider of innovative solutions that help businesses achieve their goals and drive sustainable growth."

After: "We made this for the moment you finally find exactly what you were looking for and realize you've been settling for less your whole life."

Sounds Like

"There is a version of this that is just functional. And then there is what we make. The difference is in the first breath."

Does Not Sound Like

"We're passionate about creating meaningful connections and delivering exceptional experiences that resonate with our valued customers."

(Passionate. Meaningful connections. Resonate. These are Lover words being used as filler instead of feeling. The Lover's voice puts you somewhere specific. "Valued customers" is not somewhere specific. It is a category.)

The Most Common Mistake

Generic sentimentality. The Lover's emotional register is high. When the emotion is specific and earned, it is extraordinarily powerful. When it is vague and aspirational, it tips into the kind of soft-focus brand language that everyone ignores. The antidote is always detail. The specific moment. The exact sensation. The particular person. Specificity is what separates the Lover from the brand that simply wants to feel warm.

Rewrite Challenge

Generic: "We believe in the power of human connection and are committed to creating products that bring joy and meaning to everyday moments."

Make it sensory. Make it specific. Put the reader somewhere real.

THE JESTER

"Serious brands are seriously boring."

Voice Profile

The Jester's voice is fast, unexpected, and funny in a way that makes a point. The rhythm is comedic: setup, subversion, landing. The vocabulary mixes registers in surprising ways, the formal word dropped into the casual sentence, the absurd next to the sincere. The Jester delights in the gap between what's expected and what's delivered.

Crucially: the humor is in service of truth. The Jester is not funny for its own sake. It is funny because funny is the most honest and disarming way to say what needs to be said.

The Rewrite

Before: "We are a leading provider of innovative solutions that help businesses achieve their goals and drive sustainable growth."

After: "We make software. It works. You won't cry while using it, which in this industry is genuinely not a given."

Sounds Like

"Our competitor calls their product a 'paradigm-shifting ecosystem.' We call ours 'the thing that actually does what you bought it for.' Tomato, tomato."

Does Not Sound Like

"We inject fun and energy into everything we do because we believe that work should be as enjoyable as it is productive! 😊"

(The exclamation point. The emoji. The word "inject." The idea that enthusiasm is the same as wit. Jester brands are funny because they are observant and honest. This is a brand trying to seem fun, which is the farthest possible distance from being funny.)

The Most Common Mistake

Performing humor instead of having it. Real wit is dangerous. It picks a target, makes a point, and accepts that not everyone will find it funny. The brand that wants to seem "fun and playful" without actually committing to anything funny ends up with exclamation points and emojis where a real Jester would have a punchline. The Jester earns its laughs. It does not beg for them.

Rewrite Challenge

Generic: "At the heart of everything we do is a deep commitment to our customers and a passion for excellence in every interaction."

Make it funny. Find the absurdity in the sentence first. Then say the true thing through it.

THE ORDER FAMILY

THE CAREGIVER

"We've got you."

Voice Profile

The Caregiver's voice is warm, steady, and specific to the person reading. It makes the reader feel seen before it makes them feel sold to. The rhythm is unhurried and clear, never complicated, never showing off. The vocabulary is plain and human. The Caregiver uses "you" more than any other pronoun, because the work is about the person on the other end, not the brand doing the caring.

The relationship with the reader is one of accompaniment. The Caregiver does not tell you what to do. It shows up with what you need before you have to ask.

The Rewrite

Before: "We are a leading provider of innovative solutions that help businesses achieve their goals and drive sustainable growth."

After: "You've been handling too much on your own. We know. That's exactly why we built this."

Sounds Like

"We designed this for the Wednesday afternoon when everything is going wrong at once and you need it to just work. It does."

Does Not Sound Like

"Our world-class support team is dedicated to maximizing your success metrics and ensuring optimal outcomes across all touchpoints."

(World-class. Maximizing. Optimal outcomes. Touchpoints. The Caregiver's warmth evaporated the moment those words arrived. The Caregiver sounds like a person. A person who cares. Not a vendor optimizing your outcomes at scale.)

The Most Common Mistake

Warmth without specificity. The Caregiver brand that says it cares, without demonstrating exactly what that care looks like and when, produces content that feels like a form letter from a very well-meaning organization. Care is shown in the specific: the thing you did when no one was watching, the policy that protects the customer even when it costs you, the moment you showed up. Describe that. That is the Caregiver's most powerful content.

Rewrite Challenge

Generic: "Our experienced team provides comprehensive support services to help organizations navigate complex challenges and achieve their objectives."

Make it warm. Make it specific. Put a real person in it.

THE CREATOR

"Make your mark."

Voice Profile

The Creator's voice is precise and kinetic about craft. It notices things other brands don't notice. The quality of the material, the elegance of the process, the specific decision that made the thing better. The rhythm reflects the making: iterative, building, occasionally stepping back to assess. The vocabulary is specific to the work: makers, craft, build, shape, design, iteration, the thing that almost worked and why the next version does.

The Creator writes about creation with the authority of someone who has done it, not someone who admires it from a distance.

The Rewrite

Before: "We are a leading provider of innovative solutions that help businesses achieve their goals and drive sustainable growth."

After: "We spent three years building the tool we couldn't find anywhere else. The thing you've been trying to approximate with spreadsheets and workarounds. Here it is."

Sounds Like

"Every decision in here was made on purpose. The ones that look effortless took the longest."

Does Not Sound Like

"We are passionate creators who believe in the transformative power of innovation to inspire and empower the next generation of creative thinkers."

(The Creator does not talk about creation in the abstract. It talks about making a specific thing and why every choice in it matters. "Next generation of creative thinkers" is a brand deck slide. The Creator's voice is in the work, not above it.)

The Most Common Mistake

Romanticizing craft instead of demonstrating it. The Creator archetype loves the idea of making things well. The voice failure is talking about the love of craft without showing the craft. Every Creator brand has access to a more powerful story: the specific thing they made, the specific problem it solved, the specific decision that was harder but right. That specificity is the voice. Everything else is just a mood board.

Rewrite Challenge

Generic: "We offer a full suite of customizable products and services designed to meet the evolving needs of modern businesses."

Show the craft. Show the specific decision. Make it feel made, not manufactured.

THE RULER

"Take control."

Voice Profile

The Ruler's voice is authoritative and unhurried. It does not explain itself. It states. The rhythm is measured and deliberate, every sentence earning its place. The vocabulary is precise, elevated, and free of slang. The Ruler does not use exclamation points. It does not ask questions. It makes declarations. The relationship with the reader is one of confident guidance: you are in the right hands, and the Ruler does not need to say so because it is evident.

The Rewrite

Before: "We are a leading provider of innovative solutions that help businesses achieve their goals and drive sustainable growth."

After: "The standard in this category has been inadequate. We corrected that."

Sounds Like

"Excellence is not a value proposition. It is a requirement. We have never offered anything else."

Does Not Sound Like

"We're super excited to share our latest innovative features that will totally revolutionize the way you work and help you crush your goals!"

(The Ruler does not get excited publicly. It does not "totally" anything. It does not use exclamation points. And "crush your goals" is the Hero's language, not the Ruler's. The Ruler sets the standard. It does not celebrate your goals. It expects them.)

The Most Common Mistake

Coldness as a proxy for authority. The Ruler's restraint can tip into aloofness that keeps the reader at arm's length in a way that feels less authoritative and more defensive. The best Ruler brands are warm in their certainty: they have the confidence that allows them to be human without being casual. The standard is held. The welcome is genuine. Both things are possible.

Rewrite Challenge

Generic: "We partner with organizations to develop strategic solutions that optimize performance and deliver measurable results across all areas of the business."

Strip out every hedge. Every vague word. Say it like you mean it and don't need to prove it.

THE BELONGING FAMILY

THE EVERYPERSON

"Just like you."

Voice Profile

The Everyperson's voice is conversational, specific, and free of pretension. It sounds like a text from a trusted friend who happens to know a lot. The rhythm is relaxed and natural. The vocabulary is plain, contractions are welcome, and jargon is not. The Everyperson never sounds like it's performing. It sounds like it's talking.

The relationship with the reader is horizontal. We are peers. The Everyperson is not above, ahead, or smarter. It is alongside, and that is exactly why it is trusted.

The Rewrite

Before: "We are a leading provider of innovative solutions that help businesses achieve their goals and drive sustainable growth."

After: "It does what you need it to do. Works the way you'd expect. And when something goes wrong, we pick up the phone."

Sounds Like

"We're not the flashiest option. We're the one that's still working on a Tuesday when everything else fell apart."

Does Not Sound Like

"As a purpose-driven organization committed to democratizing access to enterprise-grade capabilities, we empower everyday users to achieve extraordinary outcomes."

(Purpose-driven. Democratizing. Enterprise-grade. Extraordinary outcomes. The Everyperson archetype has been buried under six layers of positioning language. The Everyperson sounds like a person. Not a category positioning statement.)

The Most Common Mistake

Blandness disguised as relatability. The Everyperson's commitment to being accessible and approachable can flatten into having nothing distinctive to say. Relatable is not the same as forgettable. The Everyperson still has a point of view. It still has opinions. It still chooses specific words. It just doesn't make you feel small for not already knowing what they are. Find the specific thing you believe and say it plainly. That is the Everyperson voice at its best.

Rewrite Challenge

Generic: "We provide flexible, affordable solutions for small and medium-sized businesses looking to grow their operations and improve their bottom line."

Make it real. Make it human. Make it sound like someone you'd actually want to call.

THE SAGE

"Truth over trend. Clarity over chaos."

Voice Profile

The Sage's voice is precise, measured, and earned. Every claim is supported. Every assertion points to something real. The rhythm builds methodically from observation to implication to conclusion. The vocabulary is accurate over impressive: the Sage chooses the right word, not the big one. The Sage does not tell you what to think. It gives you what you need to think clearly.

The relationship with the reader is that of a trusted expert who genuinely wants the reader to understand, not just to believe.

The Rewrite

Before: "We are a leading provider of innovative solutions that help businesses achieve their goals and drive sustainable growth."

After: "Three things determine whether a business survives the next five years. We built our entire platform around two of them. Here is why, and here is the data."

Sounds Like

"The popular answer to this question is wrong. Here is what the evidence actually shows."

Does Not Sound Like

"As thought leaders in the space, we leverage our deep expertise and proprietary insights to deliver best-in-class guidance to our valued partners."

(Thought leaders. Deep expertise. Proprietary insights. Best-in-class. The Sage's authority comes from demonstrating knowledge, not from labeling itself knowledgeable. The Sage that calls itself a thought leader has usually not thought very hard about the sentence it just wrote.)

The Most Common Mistake

Lecturing. The Sage's expertise is real. The failure is deploying it in a way that makes the reader feel talked at rather than equipped. The Sage's highest purpose is to give the reader clarity they could not have reached alone. When the voice loses track of the reader and starts performing expertise for its own sake, the relationship breaks down. The measure: does the reader leave smarter? Or do they leave impressed by how much you know?

Rewrite Challenge

Generic: "Our industry-leading research and data-driven approach enable us to provide actionable insights that drive meaningful business outcomes."

Show the specific insight. One thing. True and sharp. No adjectives that do the work the noun should do.

THE INNOCENT

"Keep it simple. Keep it good."

Voice Profile

The Innocent's voice is clear, warm, and honest to the point of being slightly disarming. It does not oversell. It does not use superlatives. It does not need to. The rhythm is clean and open, white space in the writing the way there is white space in a well-designed package. The vocabulary is simple, and the Innocent's power comes from the confidence to stay simple when every instinct in marketing says to add more.

The relationship with the reader is one of uncomplicated trust: we are exactly what we say we are. No fine print.

The Rewrite

Before: "We are a leading provider of innovative solutions that help businesses achieve their goals and drive sustainable growth."

After: "We make one thing. We make it well. We've been making it the same way for twelve years because it works and we haven't wanted to cut corners yet."

Sounds Like

"Good ingredients. No shortcuts. You can read everything on the label and recognize every word."

Does Not Sound Like

"We're revolutionizing the industry with our groundbreaking approach to delivering pure, authentic experiences that connect people to what truly matters."

(Revolutionizing. Groundbreaking. Truly matters. The Innocent is not trying to revolutionize anything. It is trying to make the good thing with care and let the goodness speak. The second it starts using revolution language, it has lost the thread entirely.)

The Most Common Mistake

Naivety that ignores complexity. The Innocent's simplicity is a strength. It becomes a liability when the brand uses it to avoid honest reckoning with the harder parts of its world. The most compelling Innocent brands hold their standards with clarity about how difficult that actually is. "We use only organic ingredients" is stronger when followed by "which is expensive and sometimes means we say no to distribution deals we'd like to take." The Innocent's honesty is its power. Use all of it.

Rewrite Challenge

Generic: "We are committed to transparency, sustainability, and building products our customers can feel good about using every day."

Strip it down. Say the one true thing. No "committed to." No "feel good about." Say what you actually do and why you actually do it.

The Rewrite Exercise as a Team Workshop

This chapter works as a solo exercise. It also works better as a group one.

Here is how to run it with your team in 60 minutes or less.

Step 1: Pull three to five pieces of your worst existing copy. The most generic. The most committee-approved. The stuff that got published because it didn't offend anyone, not because it was good.

Step 2: Have everyone rewrite one piece in your brand's primary archetype. No discussion beforehand. No collaborative editing. Each person writes their version independently.

Step 3: Read them out loud. All of them. No attribution.

Step 4: Notice where they converge and where they diverge. Convergence is where your team instinctively understands the voice. Divergence is where the voice is unclear or contested. Both are information.

Step 5: Build a composite from the best of each. Not by averaging. By choosing. The sentence that is most on-voice wins, regardless of whose it is.

Do this exercise quarterly. Your voice will sharpen faster than any style guide will achieve, because the people who write for your brand will be building a shared understanding from the inside out, not following rules from the outside in.

The Final Test

At the end of every piece of content you write, run this:

Remove the logo. Remove your name. Read it out loud.

Does it sound like your archetype?

Does it sound like a specific person with a specific point of view?

Would someone who knows your brand recognize it?

If yes to all three: ship it.

If not: go back to the Voice Ingredients. Check the recipe. Find what's missing and add it.

Your archetype is the identity. Your voice is how that identity shows up in language. This chapter is the proof that they are the same thing expressed two different ways.

Know who you are. Write like it. Every time.

Brand Deck Connection: Voice + Tone Cards.

Each archetype's voice profile in this chapter corresponds directly to the front of its Brand Deck Archetype Card. The back of each card includes the voice exercise and the "sounds like / does not sound like" examples. Use them to brief writers, calibrate content, and run the rewrite workshop.

Next: Part Four. Know Your People.

Chapter 10: Your Brand Is Not for Everyone. And that's the point.

CHAPTER 10:
Your Brand Is Not for Everyone (And That's the Point)

"If you try to be everything to everyone, you'll be nothing to no one."
- Unknown (but pretty damn smart)

THE TEXTBOOK VERSION

Marketers understand that consumers buy products consistent with their self-concept. People generally purchase what matches or blends with who they think they are and who they want to be. Self-concept is listed as one of several personal factors that influence buying behavior, alongside age, occupation, economic situation, and lifestyle. It appears as a subsection. A useful data point. One bullet in a long list.

THE FIELD VERSION

Stop.

That sentence is not a bullet point. It is not a personal factor among several. It is not one data point in a long list.

It is the entire argument.

Consumers buy products consistent with their self-concept.

People do not buy features. They buy mirrors. They buy the version of themselves they want to believe in. The version they are building toward. The version they need confirmed by the brands they choose to be associated with.

The brand that best reflects a person's self-concept — their identity, their values, their aspirations, the story they are telling themselves about who they are — wins. Not sometimes. Always.

This is not a segment of the marketing equation.

This is the equation.

And the textbook buried it in a bullet point and moved on.

This chapter doesn't move on.

The Mirror Problem

Think about the last brand you became genuinely loyal to.

Not satisfied with. Loyal. The kind where you recommend it without being asked, where you feel mildly defensive when someone criticizes it, where you have told the origin story to other people at least once.

Now ask yourself: what does choosing that brand say about who you are?

Probably something real. Something you'd want said about you. Something that reflects a value, an aesthetic, an identity you're either claiming or aspiring toward.

That is the self-concept at work. It is not rational. It operates below the level of conscious feature evaluation. And it is far more powerful than any value proposition you have ever written.

The Harley-Davidson owner is not making a transportation decision. They are making an identity decision. The Patagonia buyer is not making an outerwear decision. They are making a values decision. The person who buys Moleskine notebooks over cheaper alternatives is not making a stationery decision. They are making a decision about the kind of person who shows up to take notes.

None of these decisions survive a purely rational analysis. That is the point. They are not rational. They are identity-driven. And identity-driven decisions are the most durable, repeat-purchase, word-of-mouth, price-inelastic decisions in commerce.

The brand that earns identity-level loyalty has won something that a competitor cannot take away with a feature update or a price cut.

The Specificity Trap

Here is what founders and marketers do when they hear this.

They nod. They agree. And then they write marketing copy for everyone.

Because specificity is terrifying.

What if we say this is for restaurant operators and we lose the hospitality consultants? What if we commit to the challenger brand and the enterprise buyers think we're not mature enough? What if we get too specific and someone who would have been a great customer reads the first line and decides it's not for them?

These are real fears. They are also wrong.

Here is what actually happens when you get specific: the right people recognize themselves. Immediately and viscerally. They feel found. They lean in. They share the thing because it articulates something they have been trying to articulate themselves. The specificity is not a filter keeping people out. It is a signal pulling the right people in.

And here is what happens when you are not specific: nobody recognizes themselves. The copy lands like a notification from an app they don't remember installing. Technically received. Immediately dismissed. The vague brand that tries to be for everyone becomes the brand that means nothing to anyone.

Specificity feels like risk. Vagueness feels like safety. The market teaches you otherwise, but usually too late and too slowly for the lesson to be obvious.

Demographics Are Dead. Psychographics Aren't.

The standard marketing response to audience clarity is the demographic persona.

Meet Jennifer. Jennifer is 34-45, college-educated, household income of $85-120K, two kids, suburban, digitally active, health-conscious. Jennifer enjoys outdoor activities and values quality over price.

Jennifer is fiction.

Not because the demographic cluster doesn't exist. It does. It is because Jennifer tells you nothing about what Jennifer believes, what she fears, what story she is telling herself, what kind of brand she would feel proud to be associated with, and what kind of brand would make her feel seen in a way that unlocks real loyalty.

Demographics describe what people look like from the outside. Psychographics describe what they look like from the inside. And inside is where the purchase decision actually lives.

The questions that matter are not:

- How old are they?
- What is their income?
- Where do they live?

The questions that matter are:

- What do they believe that most people in their world don't?
- What are they quietly afraid of?
- Who do they want to become?
- What would they never do, and why?
- What brands do they already love, and what does that say about them?
- What is the story they are telling themselves about their life right now?

These questions produce an audience picture that is infinitely more useful. Because these are the questions your archetype already has answers to. The Rebel's natural audience believes the system is rigged. The Sage's natural audience is afraid of being wrong. The Innocent's natural audience is tired of complexity and wants something it can trust without reading the fine print.

Your archetype is magnetized. It naturally attracts the people who share its worldview. Your job is not to figure out how to appeal to everyone. Your job is to understand your natural audience deeply enough to speak directly to the worldview they already have.

Your Natural Audience by Archetype

Every archetype has a natural audience. A type of person who is pre-wired to respond to its worldview.

This is not a rigid rule. It is a useful pattern. Know it. Use it. Then find the specific version of it in your market.

The Rebel attracts the rule-questioners, the system-distrusters, the people who have been burned by the establishment and are done pretending otherwise. They are allergic to corporate speak and they have excellent bullshit detectors. They want a brand that names what's broken and means it.

The Explorer attracts the restless, the curious, the people who are unsatisfied with the consensus answer and want to know what's over the ridge. They distrust the well-worn path not because it's wrong but because it's crowded. They want a brand that has actually gone somewhere and brought something back.

The Magician attracts the believers in possibility, the people who are not yet where they want to be and are looking for the thing that makes the transformation feel real rather than theoretical. They are drawn to brands that promise change and can prove it.

The Hero attracts the people who want to be challenged. The ones who are uncomfortable with comfortable. They want a brand that treats them as capable of more, that does not coddle, that expects effort and doesn't apologize for it.

The Lover attracts the sensory and emotional, the people who feel deeply and want the things they buy to reflect that depth. They are not impressed by specs. They are impressed by the experience of the thing, the feeling of the encounter, the way the brand makes them feel about themselves.

The Jester attracts the people who are tired of taking everything so seriously, who find most brands exhausting in their earnestness, who will give their loyalty to the brand that makes them laugh in a way that also tells the truth. They are smart and they use humor as a filter for intelligence.

The Caregiver attracts the people who are looking for a brand they can actually trust to show up. They have been let down before. They are not looking for the flashiest option. They are looking for the one that will still be there at 10pm when something goes wrong.

The Creator attracts the makers and the builders, the people who are doing something with their hands and their minds and want tools worthy of what they're building. They have high standards for craft and they extend those standards to the brands they work with.

The Ruler attracts the people who have made it and want their brands to reflect that. They are not price-sensitive. They are quality-sensitive. They want to be in the right hands, and the confidence of the Ruler's voice is what tells them they are.

The Everyperson attracts the people who are tired of brands talking down to them, performing aspiration at them, making them feel like they are not enough unless they buy the thing. They want a brand that treats them as intelligent adults who do not need to be impressed.

The Sage attracts the people who want to understand, not just be told. They will do the reading. They will follow the footnote. They want a brand that respects their intelligence and gives them something real to work with.

The Innocent attracts the people who have been let down by complexity and want to believe, once more, that something can just be what it says it is. They are not naive. They are tired. And they want a brand they can trust without conditions.

You Are Not Converting Skeptics

Here is a strategic reframe that changes everything.

You are not trying to convert skeptics. You are trying to find believers and give them a flag.

The skeptic is not your audience. The skeptic is someone whose worldview does not align with your archetype's worldview. You can spend enormous amounts of time and money trying to convince them. You will occasionally succeed. The lifetime value of that converted skeptic is almost always lower than the lifetime value of the natural believer who found you easily and immediately felt at home.

The natural believer already agrees with you. They already see the world the way your archetype sees it. They have been waiting, often without knowing it, for a brand that confirms their worldview. When they find you, they do not need convincing. They need a flag to carry.

Your job is not conversion. Your job is clarity. Be so specific and honest about who you are and what you believe that the natural believers find you faster, and the skeptics self-select out before you waste each other's time.

This feels counterintuitive in a world that optimizes for reach. But reach without resonance is noise. The thousand people who feel found by your brand are worth more than the ten thousand who vaguely remember seeing it.

The Tribe Is Not a Metaphor

Brand community is a real thing. It has real economic value.

The brands with the most durable market positions, the ones that survive downturns and category disruption and competitive pressure, are almost always the ones with genuine communities built around a shared identity.

Harley-Davidson has the HOG. Nike has its running communities and its athletes. Patagonia has the environmental activists who see the brand as a fellow traveler, not a vendor. Peloton, at its peak, had something that looked like a religion. Coke people, Pepsi people. Gibson people, Fender people. Dunkin people, Starbucks people.

These communities are not the product of a community strategy. They are the product of a brand that had a clear enough archetype and a specific enough worldview that the people who shared that worldview found each other around the brand.

The archetype creates the gravity. The gravity creates the gathering. The gathering creates the community. The community creates the moat.

You do not build a brand community. You build a brand with a clear enough identity that a community builds itself around it.

Your audience clarity is the first step. You cannot attract your tribe if you do not know who they are and speak directly to them. Vague brands do not create communities. They create mailing lists.

The Exclusion Principle

Choosing your audience means un-choosing others. That is not a failure. That is the strategy.

The most common fear in this conversation is the fear of exclusion. What if we lose someone? What if someone reads our positioning and decides it's not for them?

The reframe: exclusion is how you make the included feel included.

When a brand is clearly not for everyone, the people it is for feel it. They feel the specificity. They feel the recognition. They feel the slight self-satisfaction of belonging to the group that gets it.

This is not elitism. It is just how identity works. We all want to belong somewhere specific, not somewhere general. A community that will take anyone isn't really a community. A brand that's for everyone isn't really for you.

The Rebel brand that is clearly not for the corporate conformist makes the non-conformist feel seen. The Sage brand that is clearly not for the person who wants to be told what to think makes the independent thinker feel respected. The Innocent brand that is clearly not for the cynical makes the idealist feel like there is somewhere safe for them.

Un-choose loudly. The people you are choosing will notice.

Radical Audience Clarity

The goal of this chapter is not a persona. It is clarity.

Clarity about who your brand is for at the identity level.

Not age and income. Identity. Values. Worldview. The story they are telling themselves. What they believe that most people don't. What they are moving toward. What they are leaving behind.

The brand that has this clarity writes better copy. Builds better products. Hires better people. Makes better decisions faster, because it always knows who the decision is being made for.

The brand that lacks this clarity second-guesses everything. The copy sounds like it was written for no one because it was written for everyone. The product roadmap is pulled in ten directions because there is no clear center of gravity. The marketing spend diffuses across channels and personas and messages and produces a lot of reach and not much resonance.

Radical audience clarity is not a nice-to-have. It is a structural requirement. You cannot build an identity-led brand without knowing whose identity you are trying to reflect.

That knowledge lives in Chapter 11. Eight tools from the Brand Deck, each one designed to get you past the demographic surface and into the psychographic truth of who your natural audience actually is.

Brand Deck Connection: Summary Card 4, Audience Insights.

The overview of all eight Audience Insight tools, with the single most important question for each one. Start here. Then go deep in Chapter 11.

Next: Chapter 11. The 8 Audience Insight Cards.

Eight tools for understanding who you're actually speaking to.

CHAPTER 11:
The 8 Audience Insight Cards

"You can't sell anything if you can't tell anything."

-- Beth Comstock

Eight tools.

Each one gets you past the surface of who your audience is. Past the demographic profile, the age range, the job title, the income bracket. Into the actual human territory: what they believe, what they fear, what they want to become, and what story they are telling themselves that your brand either confirms or ignores.

For each tool you get the framework, how to use it, what it produces, and an activation that turns the exercise into something real.

These work alone. They work better in combination. Run all eight over time and you will have a more complete picture of your natural audience than any market research report has ever given you.

CARD 1: The Belief Inventory

"What do they believe that most people don't?"

What It Is

An inventory of the unconventional beliefs your natural audience holds. Not their stated preferences, their actual convictions: the things they think are true that most people in their world would push back on.

Unconventional beliefs are the most powerful signal of identity alignment. People who share an unusual belief feel an immediate, disproportionate bond with a brand that names it. The recognition is almost physical. "They get it. They actually get it."

How to Use It

Start with your own archetype's worldview. What does your archetype believe? What would it argue with? What would it refuse to accept as conventional wisdom?

Then translate that into the audience's version. If your brand is a Rebel that believes the industry is running a quiet racket on its customers, your natural audience believes they've been paying for something they were never getting. Name that belief specifically.

Some prompts:

- What does your best customer believe about your category that your average customer doesn't?
- What does your best customer think is wrong with how most brands in your space operate?
- What would your natural audience say if they were being completely honest at the end of a long day?

The Output

A list of three to five specific, uncomfortable, true beliefs that your natural audience holds. Not values. Not preferences. Beliefs. "Operators don't need another dashboard, they need someone who has actually worked a Saturday night service." "Most HR software is designed for the company, not for the employee." "The best coffee in the world is not available in most of the places where people drink coffee."

Specific. Uncomfortable. True.

Why It Matters for Archetype

Each archetype's natural audience has a predictable belief set. The Sage's audience believes truth is more valuable than comfort. The Hero's audience believes that most people don't work hard enough and that effort is underrated. The Caregiver's audience believes that most organizations don't actually care as much as they claim. Know the belief cluster and you know the door.

Activation

Interview your three best customers. Not about features. Ask them: "What do you believe about this industry that most people get wrong?" Record the answers verbatim. The patterns in those answers are your Belief Inventory.

CARD 2: The Fear Map

"What keeps them up at 3am?"

What It Is

A structured inventory of your audience's real fears. Not the surface fears they mention in polite company. The ones at 3am. The ones that shape decisions without ever being named in a sales conversation.

Fear is a primary purchase driver. Not the only one, but one of the most honest. Understanding what your audience is genuinely afraid of is not manipulation. It is empathy at scale. It is the difference between a brand that speaks to the situation the customer is presenting and a brand that speaks to the situation the customer is actually living.

How to Use It

Fear operates at three levels, and each level is more useful than the one above it.

Surface fear: The stated problem. "I'm worried about my marketing ROI." "I need better customer retention numbers." "Our HR costs are too high."

Real fear: What's underneath the stated problem. "I'm worried that what we've been doing isn't working and I don't know what to do instead." "I'm afraid the churn is telling me something about the product I don't want to hear." "I'm afraid I've built a team that can't scale."

Identity fear: The deepest level. "I'm afraid I'm not as good at this as I thought I was." "I'm afraid my team sees it too." "I'm afraid we're building something that doesn't matter and I've been lying to myself about it."

Your messaging can operate at any level. The deeper you go, the more resonant and the more trust required to get there. Know all three levels. Calibrate to the right one for the right moment.

The Output

A Fear Map with at least two fears at each level: surface, real, and identity. This becomes the brief for messaging that meets the customer where they actually are, not where they are pretending to be.

Why It Matters for Archetype

The Caregiver's messaging operates primarily at the real fear level: acknowledging what is underneath the stated problem and offering steady reassurance. The Hero's messaging often operates at the identity fear level: naming the gap between who the customer is and who they could be, then making that gap feel closeable. The Sage's messaging operates at the surface and real fear levels, giving the audience the clarity and information they need to stop being afraid of something they now understand.

Know your archetype's natural fear register and you know where your messaging is most effective.

Activation

Look at your last ten customer conversations, sales calls, support tickets, or reviews. For each one, identify the stated fear and then ask: what is the fear underneath that? Do it once more. Go one level deeper. The identity fear is rarely stated. It is implied. Learn to read the implication.

CARD 3: The Aspiration Portrait

"Who are they becoming?"

What It Is

A portrait of who your natural audience is actively trying to become. Not who they are today. The future self they are building toward, consciously or not.

Self-concept is not static. It is directional. People are always moving toward some version of themselves: more successful, more respected, more free, more creative, more in control, more at peace. The brand that reflects the destination of that journey, not just the current location, creates a pull that demographic targeting cannot produce.

How to Use It

Start with the aspiration that your archetype naturally activates.

The Hero's audience is becoming stronger, more capable, more willing to do the hard thing. The Sage's audience is becoming wiser, more informed, more able to navigate complexity with confidence. The Explorer's audience is becoming more adventurous, more independent, more willing to go off the marked path. The Lover's audience is becoming more sensory, more alive, more present to the richness of their own experience.

Then get specific. The aspiration in your category, for your specific natural audience.

Some prompts:

- If your best customer's life looked exactly the way they want it to in three years, what would be different?
- Who do they admire? What qualities do they most want to embody?
- What would they have to believe about themselves to feel like they've made it?

The Output

An Aspiration Portrait: a two-paragraph description of the future self your natural audience is moving toward. Written as a person, not a demographic. Specific enough to brief creative work. True enough to recognize.

Why This Changes Messaging

Most brands message to who the audience is. The brands with the deepest loyalty message to who the audience is becoming. Peloton didn't sell you a bike. It sold you the version of yourself that gets up at 5:30 and does the work. Duolingo doesn't sell you a language app. It sells you the version of yourself that actually speaks another language.

You are not selling a product. You are offering a mirror that reflects the person they're building. Get that image right and you have something no feature list can compete with.

Activation

Ask your three best customers: "Who are you trying to become? Not professionally. As a person." The answers will surprise you. And they will tell you more about your brand's real positioning than any market research report ever will.

CARD 4: The Values Alignment Test

"What do we share that matters?"

What It Is

A structured comparison between your brand's values, the convictions expressed through your archetype, and the values of your natural audience. The goal is to find genuine overlap and name it explicitly.

Values alignment is the foundation of identity-level loyalty. When a customer believes their brand shares their values, the relationship becomes something closer to alliance than transaction. They are not just buying a product. They are investing in a worldview they want to see succeed.

How to Use It

Identify your brand's three to five non-negotiable values. Not the ones on your About page because they sounded right. The ones you would hold even if they cost you.

Then identify the values of your natural audience. What do they actually care about? Where do they put their money and their attention when no one is watching?

Test for genuine overlap. Not surface overlap, "we both care about quality" means nothing, but specific overlap. "We both believe that cutting corners in this process is a form of dishonesty. We've never done it. Our best customers have never done it either. That's not a coincidence."

The Output

A values overlap map: your brand's core values on one side, your natural audience's core values on the other, the genuine intersection in the middle. The intersection is where your brand story lives. Everything else is supporting material.

The Warning

Values alignment only works when it is real. The brand that claims shared values it doesn't hold will be found out. The audience that tests those values and finds them hollow becomes the audience that destroys trust publicly and permanently. The Innocent brand with a supply chain scandal. The Rebel brand caught playing corporate politics. The Caregiver brand that abandons its customers when it gets inconvenient.

Claim only the values you will hold under pressure. Then hold them under pressure.

Activation

Make two columns. Column one: the three values your brand would refuse to compromise even at a significant cost. Column two: the three values your best customers demonstrate through their behavior, not their words. Find the intersection. Name it in one sentence. That sentence is the heart of your brand's values story.

CARD 5: The Identity Mirror

"What does choosing us say about them?"

What It Is

A direct examination of the identity signal your brand sends when someone chooses it. What does it say about the person? What does it say to other people? What does it confirm or create about their self-concept?

Every brand choice is a statement. Conscious or not, the things we buy and the brands we align with communicate something to the world and to ourselves. The Identity Mirror makes that communication explicit so you can use it with intention.

How to Use It

Ask: if someone chose your brand over every other option in the category, what would that choice communicate?

To themselves: "I am the kind of person who..."

To others: "This person is someone who..."

To their future self: "This is consistent with who I'm becoming because..."

Now ask: is the statement your brand currently makes the statement your natural audience wants to make?

If yes: lean into it. Name it. Make the mirror clearer.

If no: there is a gap between your brand's current identity signal and the signal your natural audience is looking for. That gap is the brief.

The Output

Three sentences. One for each perspective: the self-statement, the social signal, and the future-self confirmation. Post these somewhere your marketing team can see them. Every campaign should make at least one of them more true.

Why the Jester Gets This Wrong

The Jester's audience makes an identity choice with a Jester brand: "I am the person who doesn't take things too seriously. Who finds the absurdity in the serious thing. Who has enough confidence in myself to laugh at the category I'm in." That is a specific and valuable identity signal.

Where Jester brands get this wrong: they think the identity signal is "I have a sense of humor" when actually it is "I am smart enough to find this funny." The smarter signal attracts the smarter audience. Know what your brand actually says. Not what you think it says.

Activation

Show your brand's homepage to five people who are not in your category. Ask them: "If someone you respected told you they used this brand, what would you think about them?" The answers are your current Identity Mirror, unfiltered. If the answers don't match the mirror you want to hold up, you know what needs to change.

CARD 6: The Worldview Window

"How do they see the world?"

What It Is

A structured examination of your natural audience's worldview: their fundamental assumptions about how things work, what matters, what's possible, and who to trust. Worldview is the lens through which all information is filtered, including your brand's messaging. Understand the lens and you understand what lands.

How to Use It

Worldview operates at several levels. All of them matter.

Category worldview: How does your audience think about the category your brand operates in? Do they trust it? Distrust it? Have they been burned? Are they skeptical of solutions or hungry for them?

Industry worldview: If your audience is in an industry, how do they see that industry? What do they believe about its future? Its problems? Its potential?

Life worldview: The broadest level. Is your natural audience fundamentally optimistic or realistic? Do they believe effort produces results? Do they trust institutions? Do they see complexity as manageable or overwhelming?

The Rebel's natural audience has a worldview shaped by distrust of power and appreciation for those who call it out. The Innocent's natural audience has a worldview shaped by a desire for things to be as good as they say they are, and a guardedness born from times they weren't. The Sage's natural audience has a worldview where the right information, honestly delivered, can solve almost any problem.

The Output

A Worldview Window: three paragraphs describing how your natural audience sees the world, the category, and the problem your brand solves. Written in their voice, not yours. This becomes the empathy foundation for every piece of messaging you build.

Activation

Read the forums, subreddits, Slack groups, and LinkedIn threads where your natural audience congregates. Read without an agenda. Just listen. What are the recurring frustrations? The recurring beliefs? The things that keep coming up in different words? That is your audience's worldview, expressed at scale in their own language.

CARD 7: The Belonging Signal

"Where do they feel at home?"

What It Is

An inventory of the communities, references, and cultural signals that make your natural audience feel recognized and at home. The places they gather, the things they care about, the references that land, the signals that say "you are in the right place."

Belonging is one of the deepest human drives. The brand that makes its natural audience feel like they belong somewhere specific builds a relationship that goes far beyond transaction. They are not just customers. They are members.

How to Use It

Ask: where does your natural audience already gather? Online and offline. What are they reading? Watching? Attending? Participating in? What podcasts do they listen to? What accounts do they follow? What events make them feel like they are with their people?

Then ask: what cultural references does your brand make that land with this audience? What references do you avoid because they feel off? What shared language have you developed with your best customers?

The Belonging Signal is about making the right people feel at home the moment they encounter your brand. The specific reference. The knowing shorthand. The proof that you are from the same world.

The Output

A Belonging Signal inventory: the communities, references, events, language, and cultural markers that your natural audience uses to recognize each other. This becomes the creative brief for content that makes the right people feel found.

A Practical Application

If you are in restaurant technology and your natural audience is independent operators, you know the belonging signals. The jokes about the 86 board. The references to Sunday prep. The shorthand around labor costs and the particular exhaustion of a Saturday night that doesn't go the way it was supposed to. The brand that speaks that language has already done more relationship-building than a brand that lists its features could do in a hundred sales calls.

Speak the language of the community. Not as a performance. As a genuine resident.

Activation

List every piece of shared language, every inside reference, every community signal that your natural audience would recognize. Then audit your content. How much of it uses this language? How much of it sounds like it could have been written by anyone who has never spent a day in their world? Close that gap.

CARD 8: The Decision Trigger

"What finally makes them act?"

What It Is

An examination of the specific moment, event, or accumulation of evidence that finally triggers your natural audience to take action. Not why they are interested. Why they move.

There is a gap between interest and action. Understanding what bridges that gap is the most commercially useful insight in this chapter.

How to Use It

Decision triggers come in three forms.

The Incident: A specific event that changes the calculus. The restaurant that lost data during a server crash and finally invested in backup systems. The founder who read the wrong NPS score at the wrong moment and finally hired a brand strategist. The operator who watched a competitor's brand become the one customers talked about and realized they had been ignoring the thing that mattered.

The Accumulation: No single event. Just enough small confirmations of a growing belief that action becomes obvious. "I kept seeing the problem. I kept finding a way around it. Then one day I stopped finding the workaround and just decided to fix it."

The Permission: The audience knew what they needed to do. They were waiting for something to tell them it was okay to do it. A peer's recommendation. A case study of someone like them making the move. A piece of content that named the problem they had been afraid to admit and said "this is fixable."

The Output

A Decision Trigger profile for your natural audience: which type of trigger most commonly moves them, what the trigger typically looks like in your category, and what your brand can do to be present at that moment.

Why This Matters More Than You Think

Most marketing is designed to create awareness and interest. It almost never thinks about the decision trigger. The brand that understands what finally moves its audience can engineer for that moment. It can build the case study that serves as permission. It can create the content that names the accumulation. It can be in the right place at the moment of the incident.

Awareness is necessary. It is not sufficient. The audience that is aware of your brand and never moves is just a mailing list. The audience that moves is the one that encountered your brand at the right moment with the right trigger.

Activation

Ask your last ten customers: "What finally made you decide to move on this?" Listen for the pattern. Then ask: "What would have made you move sooner?" The gap between those two answers is the most valuable thing your sales and marketing team is currently not acting on.

Putting the Eight Cards Together

Each card illuminates a different dimension of your natural audience.

- ☐ The Belief Inventory tells you what they think.
- ☐ The Fear Map tells you what they feel.
- ☐ The Aspiration Portrait tells you where they're going.
- ☐ The Values Alignment Test tells you what you share.
- ☐ The Identity Mirror tells you what choosing you says about them.
- ☐ The Worldview Window tells you how they see the world.
- ☐ The Belonging Signal tells you where they feel at home.
- ☐ The Decision Trigger tells you what finally makes them move.

Together, they build something no demographic profile has ever built: a complete picture of a human being whose worldview aligns with your brand, whose identity is reflected in your archetype, and whose decision you can finally engineer for.

That is not a target audience. That is a tribe.

And in Chapter 12, you learn how to connect that tribe to your archetype in a way that makes every piece of messaging you produce feel like it was written specifically for them.

Because it was.

Brand Deck Connection: Audience Insight Cards 1-8.

Each card in this chapter has a corresponding Brand Deck card with the key question, a workshop prompt, and a space for your specific audience answers. Run the full set in a half-day session with your marketing team. What comes out will be more useful than any agency research brief you have ever received.

Next: Chapter 12. Matching Archetype to Audience.

Your identity and your audience's identity. The bridge between them is where your brand actually lives.

CHAPTER 12:
Matching Archetype to Audience

"The right message to the wrong person is noise. The right message to the right person is recognition."

You have two things now.

You have an archetype. The identity at the core of your brand. The character you are at the bone, expressed in the way you write, the story you tell, the voice you show up with.

You have an audience picture. Not a demographic. A human portrait: what they believe, what they fear, where they are going, what they share with you, what finally makes them move.

Neither one works alone.

A perfectly defined archetype with no understanding of its natural audience is a brilliant brand that nobody finds. It speaks the right language in an empty room. The conviction is real. The articulation is sharp. Nobody is listening.

A perfectly researched audience with no clear brand identity is a well-targeted message with nothing to say. You know exactly who you're talking to. You have nothing worth saying to them.

The bridge between the two is where your brand actually lives.

This chapter builds that bridge.

The Alignment Principle

Your archetype and your audience are aligned when the story your brand tells is the story your audience is already telling themselves.

Not a version of it. Not a flattering reflection of it. The same story.

The Rebel brand and its natural audience share a story: the system is failing the people it claims to serve, and the right response is refusal, not accommodation. When a Rebel brand names that story precisely, the natural audience does not feel marketed to. They feel recognized. The brand did not create the belief. The brand found it, named it, and gave it a home.

The Caregiver brand and its natural audience share a story: you shouldn't have to handle this alone, and the right response from someone who has the means to help is to show up. When a Caregiver brand demonstrates that story through consistent action, the natural audience does not just buy the product. They become advocates, because the brand is living proof that the thing they believe about how people should treat each other is actually possible in a commercial context.

This is alignment. The brand's story and the audience's story rhyming so clearly that the connection feels inevitable.

The test for alignment is simple: when your ideal customer reads your best piece of content, do they feel marketed to, or do they feel understood?

Marketed to is fine. Understood is loyal.

Where Alignment Breaks Down

Knowing both your archetype and your audience is not sufficient. You have to maintain the alignment as your brand grows, changes, and as the people writing for it turn over.

Alignment breaks down in three specific ways.

Voice drift without audience recalibration. As we covered in Chapter 7, brand voice drifts. When it does, the audience is the first to feel it. The Rebel brand that softens its edges to accommodate enterprise buyers loses the natural audience that loved it before it went corporate. The Jester brand that gets serious for a relaunch campaign leaves its community feeling abandoned. The drift is always the same direction: toward the safe middle. The audience always notices.

Audience evolution without brand evolution. Your natural audience is not static. They grow. Their needs change. What resonated when they were starting out may not resonate when they are established. The brand that does not evolve with its best customers eventually finds itself speaking to the version of those customers that no longer exists.

Expanding the audience at the cost of the core. The growth instinct says: we've saturated the early audience, we need to go broader. This is sometimes right. It is more often a trap. When you broaden the audience, you inevitably soften the message. When you soften the message, the core audience starts to feel like they are no longer who the brand is for. You lose the most loyal, most vocal, most influential part of your customer base in pursuit of a larger but shallower pool.

The discipline is to grow your reach without softening your identity. Which is possible. But it requires intentional effort and a willingness to hold the specificity even when the marketing instinct says to blur it.

The Messaging Bridge

Here is a practical framework for connecting archetype to audience in every piece of content you produce.

Every piece of brand communication operates at one or more of three levels.

Identity Level: Who we are. What we believe. The story we share with our natural audience. Messaging at this level creates belonging. It makes the right people feel found. It is not trying to convince anyone of anything. It is simply stating the truth of the brand's identity clearly enough that the people who share that identity recognize it.

Examples: brand manifestos, origin stories, values statements that demonstrate rather than declare, thought leadership that takes a real position.

Aspiration Level: Where we're going together. What becomes possible when our audience aligns with our brand. Messaging at this level creates pull. It connects the brand's offer to the audience's directional movement, to who they are becoming rather than who they are.

Examples: before-and-after stories, future-state copy, content that makes the transformation feel specific and real.

Decision Level: Why now. What specifically makes this the moment. Messaging at this level converts. It is not trying to create identity alignment or aspiration. It is meeting someone who already has both and helping them take the next step.

Examples: offers, case studies that speak to decision triggers, testimonials that remove the last remaining uncertainty.

Most brands operate almost entirely at the Decision Level. They wonder why conversion is hard. Conversion is hard because there is no identity or aspiration foundation underneath it. Decision Level messaging works when the other two levels have already done their job. In isolation, it just sounds like sales pressure.

The strongest brand content ladders across all three levels: it makes you feel found (identity), shows you where you could go (aspiration), and gives you a reason to move today (decision).

Archetype-Audience Pairing: Practical Guidance

Twelve archetypes. Endless variations of natural audience. Here is the essential guidance for each pairing.

Rebel — Natural Audience:

They distrust the default. Speak to what's broken. The aspiration is freedom from the thing they've been tolerating. The decision trigger is usually the incident: the moment it became impossible to keep pretending the old way was fine. Your content should make them feel like a peer, not a prospect.

Explorer — Natural Audience:

They are restless and curious. Speak to the horizon, not the safety of the known path. The aspiration is discovery. The decision trigger is accumulation: enough evidence that you have been somewhere they haven't and brought something worth having back. Your content should feel like a dispatch from the front, not a brochure from a travel agent.

Magician — Natural Audience:

They believe in transformation but have been burned by brands that promised it without delivering. Speak to the specific transformation, not the concept of it. The aspiration is the after state, made vivid enough to believe. The decision trigger is seeing someone like them make the leap. Your content should show the transformation in specific detail.

Hero — Natural Audience:

They want to be challenged. They are suspicious of easy. The aspiration is the version of themselves that did the hard thing. The decision trigger is permission: the content or community that says the standard you hold yourself to is real and achievable. Your content should feel like a coach, not a cheerleader.

Lover — Natural Audience:

They want depth and sensation. They are unmoved by specs. The aspiration is fully inhabiting an experience rather than just consuming it. The decision trigger is usually the encounter: tasting it, touching it, experiencing the first version of what the full thing feels like. Your content should create the encounter. Not describe it.

Jester — Natural Audience:

They are tired of brands that take themselves too seriously. The aspiration is the relief of laughing at the thing everyone pretends to take seriously. The decision trigger is accumulation: enough moments of genuine wit that the brand becomes part of their identity as someone who is smart and irreverent. Your content should earn the laugh and then land the point.

Caregiver — Natural Audience:

They are carrying too much. They are looking for something to trust. The aspiration is not having to handle one more thing alone. The decision trigger is the moment of overwhelm, or the recommendation from someone they trust who says "this one actually showed up." Your content should make them feel seen before it makes them feel sold to.

Creator — Natural Audience:

They have high standards for craft and they extend those standards to the tools they use. The aspiration is making the thing they are trying to make, better, faster, and with the satisfaction of craft rather than the frustration of compromise. The decision trigger is usually trying it: the first moment the tool does what they thought no tool could do. Your content should demonstrate the craft, not just describe it.

Ruler — Natural Audience:

They have made it and they want their choices to reflect that. They are not looking to be impressed. They are looking to have their taste confirmed. The aspiration is the quiet assurance of being in the right hands. The decision trigger is usually reputation: what the right people say about your brand when you're not in the room. Your content should be as assured and unshowy as the archetype itself.

Everyperson — Natural Audience:

They are tired of being talked down to. They want to be treated like intelligent adults who can make their own decisions. The aspiration is the simple satisfaction of something that just works, without the performance or the premium for a name they don't need. The decision trigger is the peer recommendation or the review that says "it's exactly what it says it is." Your content should sound like a person, not a brand.

Sage — Natural Audience:

They want to understand, not just be told what to do. They will follow the argument if you show your work. The aspiration is the confidence that comes from knowing, not just believing. The decision trigger is usually the insight: the moment when a piece of your content gives them something they could not have gotten anywhere else. Your content should make them smarter.

Innocent — Natural Audience:

They want to trust something again. They have been burned by complexity, fine print, and brands that were not what they said. The aspiration is the relief of something simple and good. The decision trigger is often the moment they read the label, the policy, the About page and it says exactly what it means with no exceptions. Your content should be as clean and honest as the product.

The One-Page Brand-Audience Brief

This is the deliverable that Chapter 12 is building toward.

One page. Every essential element. Specific enough that any writer, any designer, any agency, any AI tool can produce on-brand, on-audience content from it.

Here is the structure:

Who we are: Archetype (primary and secondary). Core belief. Voice recipe in three attributes with percentages. The one sentence that, if removed from our logo, anyone who knows us would recognize as ours.

Who we're for: The natural audience in psychographic terms. Their unconventional belief. Their real fear. Where they are going. What they share with us. What finally makes them move.

The story we share: The single sentence that articulates the worldview both the brand and the audience hold. The overlap. The thing that, when stated, makes the right person feel found.

What we make possible: The aspiration. The specific transformation. The before and after in plain language.

What we never do: The three things that are definitionally off-brand, with no exceptions.

That is the brief. One page. No abbreviations, no shortcuts, no adjective lists. Every line specific enough to write from.

If you can hand this to a writer you have never worked with and get back something that sounds like your brand, the brief is working.

If you cannot, go back to the chapter that built the element that isn't working yet and run the exercise again until it is.

The Compound Effect

Here is what happens when archetype and audience are genuinely aligned and consistently expressed over time.

The brand becomes a place people come from. Not just a vendor they use. Not just a product they buy. A reference point for their identity.

"I'm a Patagonia person." "I'm a Nike runner." "I'm an Airbnb traveler." "I use Notion."

These are identity statements. They are not product preferences. And the brands that earn them did it by being specific and consistent enough, over a long enough period, that the audience started to see themselves in the brand's mirror.

That is the compound effect of alignment. It does not happen in a quarter. It happens over years. But it is the most durable competitive advantage available. And it starts with a brand that knows who it is and an audience strategy that knows who that identity is for.

You now have both.

Part Five is where it becomes real.

Next: Part Five. Activate.

Chapter 13: Stop Planning. Start Shipping.

The last unfair advantage is worthless if it stays in the deck.

CHAPTER 13:
Stop Planning. Start Shipping.

"A good plan violently executed now is better than a perfect plan executed next week."

-- George S. Patton

THE TEXTBOOK VERSION

The marketing process ends at Step 5: capture value from customers to create profits and customer equity. After understanding the marketplace, designing strategy, constructing an integrated program, building relationships, and capturing value, the process repeats. Loop back to Step 1. Understand again. Design again. Construct again. The cycle continues.

This is a loop of analysis, planning, execution, and measurement. Run it correctly. Repeat it consistently. Win.

THE FIELD VERSION

The loop is real. The problem is that most brand strategy never enters it.

It stalls in the planning phase. Endlessly refined. Relentlessly edited. Scheduled for review in Q2, then pushed to Q3, then tabled pending the new hire, then waiting for the website redesign, then held until after the conference, then deprioritized because something urgent came up.

The brand brief becomes the brand bible.

The brand bible becomes the brand vault.

The brand vault becomes the thing nobody has opened since the agency delivered it fourteen months ago.

Meanwhile, your competitor with a rougher version of the same idea is in market. Learning. Iterating. Building the one thing you cannot buy: the compounding advantage of time spent in front of your audience.

You are still deciding. They are already adjusting.

This chapter is a manifesto on action. Not recklessness. Not ignoring the strategy work you've done. Action. The willingness to take what you know, which is now considerable, and put it in front of people who need it.

Done and learning beats perfect and paralyzed. Every time.

The Three Places Brand Strategy Gets Stuck

If you have done the work in this book and are still not shipping, it is for one of three reasons. Only three. Find yours.

Reason One: The Clarity Problem

You do not actually have the clarity you think you have.

The archetype exercise produced a primary archetype and a secondary, but when you try to write from them the voice doesn't come naturally. The audience work produced a psychographic portrait that felt right in the room and feels abstract on a Monday morning. The story frameworks make sense in theory and you haven't actually used one yet.

Clarity that doesn't produce output is incomplete clarity. It is still conceptual. It has not been tested against reality.

The fix is not more planning. The fix is a small, low-stakes piece of content. One LinkedIn post. One email to your list. One paragraph rewritten through your archetype's voice. Force the concept through the output and you will discover immediately what is clear and what is still fuzzy. The fuzz is the brief for the next hour of work. Not weeks. One hour.

Reason Two: The Permission Problem

You know what to do. You are waiting for someone to tell you it is okay to do it.

This is more common than most people admit. Founders wait for their investor to approve the brand direction. Marketing directors wait for the CEO to sign off on the voice guide. Agency clients wait for the internal alignment meeting that never quite gets scheduled.

Here is the permission: you have done the work. The archetype is right. The story is real. The audience is yours. Nothing in this book required anyone else's approval. The brand is yours. The story is yours. The voice is yours.

Ship it.

You will get feedback. Some of it will be useful. Almost none of it will require you to go back to the beginning. The feedback you get from the market is more useful than the feedback you are imagining from the committee that hasn't assembled yet.

Reason Three: The Perfectionism Problem

You know what to do. You have permission. You are waiting for the work to be good enough.

This is the hardest one because it wears the clothing of standards. It feels like caring about quality. It is actually fear dressed up as diligence.

Here is the truth about brand work: the version you ship today, which is imperfect, builds more equity than the version you ship in six months, which is also imperfect but which cost you six months of compounding.

Your brand voice gets sharper in public, not in private. The feedback loop of publishing and observing and adjusting is the only thing that makes it better. You cannot edit your way to a strong brand voice. You have to write your way there.

The first version of anything is never the best version. The only way to get to the best version is through the first one.

The Minimum Viable Brand Position

Before you can ship, you need to know what "minimum viable" actually means for brand work. Because this is not the same as shipping something half-finished.

The Minimum Viable Brand Position is not a rough draft with placeholder copy. It is the smallest complete version of your brand story that is true enough to represent you.

It has five elements. All five. No shortcuts.

One: Your primary archetype, named and expressed.

Not just identified. Actually expressed in the copy. A reader should be able to feel who this brand is after reading the first three sentences of your homepage. If they can't, you're not at minimum viable yet.

Two: Your core belief, stated plainly.

The one thing your brand believes that shapes everything else. Not a values statement. A conviction. The thing your brand would say even if it cost you a customer.

Three: Your natural audience, named specifically.

Not "small business owners." Not "restaurant professionals." The specific psychographic portrait of the person this brand is for. Specific enough that when they read your copy they feel found.

Four: Your origin, honest and brief.

Why this brand needs to exist. Not the company history. The human reason. One paragraph.

Five: A demonstration of your voice.

A piece of content — any piece — that sounds unmistakably like your archetype. The voice profile is nothing until there is content that proves it.

That is the minimum viable brand position. Five elements. All specific. All true. All expressed.

If you have all five, you are ready. Not perfect. Ready.

The Ship-It-Dirty Principle

Let's talk about "dirty."

Dirty does not mean sloppy. Dirty does not mean wrong. Dirty does not mean embarrassing.

Dirty means: not polished to the point of paralysis. Not delayed for the final revision that has been pending for three weeks. Not held for the photoshoot or the website launch or the event or the funding announcement or the season or whatever the next scheduled moment of readiness is.

The Ship-It-Dirty Principle says: if it is true, specific, and on-voice, it is ready. The polish can follow. The version 2.0 can be better. But the thing that gets shipped today and builds one day of compounding advantage is more valuable than the thing that gets shipped in a month because you waited.

Here is the Dirty Test. Three questions.

One: Is it true? Does this accurately represent what the brand actually believes and what it actually does?

Two: Is it specific? Could someone else claim this verbatim, or does it belong to your brand?

Three: Is it on-voice? Does it sound like your archetype?

Yes to all three: ship it.

No to any one of them: fix that one thing and ship it.

That is the entire framework. It is this simple. The complexity lives in the work that came before this chapter, in the identity and story and voice and audience work. If that work was done honestly, the shipping decision is not complicated.

The Compounding Advantage

Every day your brand is not in front of your audience, your competitor is.

This is not an argument for recklessness. It is an argument for urgency. For understanding that brand equity, like financial equity, compounds over time. The brand that starts building today is ahead of the brand that starts building in six months, not just by six months but by six months of learning, iteration, audience feedback, and presence.

You cannot buy back the six months you spent in the planning phase.

You cannot make up the conversations that happened in your absence.

You cannot retroactively be the brand that was there when your best prospect was first forming an opinion about this category.

Time spent in market is the most non-renewable asset in brand building. It cannot be accelerated with budget. It cannot be substituted with strategy. It accumulates only through presence.

The brand that shows up every week, even imperfectly, with something true and specific, is building something the brand that is preparing to show up cannot touch.

Speed Without Losing Yourself

There is a version of this chapter that someone reads as permission to skip the work.

Skip the archetype work. Skip the story frameworks. Skip the voice building. Skip the audience clarity. Just ship stuff fast and figure it out.

That is not what this chapter is saying.

Speed without identity is just noise produced quickly. The brand that ships constantly with no archetype clarity produces a body of work that is voluminous and forgettable. It is the brand that has been in market for three years and still cannot explain who it is or why someone should care.

The work in the first twelve chapters of this book is the prerequisite for this one.

The archetype gives you permission to move fast because you always know who you are. Every question about whether to say this thing or that thing, to take this position or that one, to use this voice or that one, is answered before it is asked. The archetype is the compass. When the compass is working, you can move quickly without getting lost.

The ship-it-dirty principle only applies to brands that know who they are. For the brands that don't, the answer is still the front of this book, not the back.

If you are here and you know your archetype, your story, your voice, and your audience: move. If you are here and you still feel fuzzy on any of those: go back and do the work. The shipping is worth nothing until the identity is real.

What Your Archetype Does When It Is Ready

Each archetype ships differently. Knowing this about your archetype saves you from shipping in the wrong channel with the wrong format at the wrong velocity.

The **Rebel** ships the provocation. The piece of content that names the thing nobody else is willing to name. They ship it publicly, unhedged, and accept the response from people who disagree. That response is signal, not noise.

The **Explorer** ships the dispatch. The finding from the journey. The thing they went looking for and found. The Explorer ships on curiosity: when they find something worth sharing, they share it. The cadence follows the discovery.

The **Magician** ships the transformation proof. The before and after. The specific demonstration that what they claim is possible is actually happening for real people. The Magician ships when the evidence is ready to show.

The **Hero** ships the challenge. The thing that makes the audience's pulse quicken. The Dare. The standard set just higher than comfortable. The Hero ships consistently because the challenge doesn't wait.

The **Lover** ships the experience. The piece of content that makes you feel something before you understand something. The Lover ships slowly and with intention. Quality and sensation over volume.

The **Jester** ships the bit. The observation that is funny because it is true. The Jester ships fast because the news cycle is the material and stale humor is the death of the archetype. If the moment passes, so does the bit.

The **Caregiver** ships the presence. The check-in. The piece of content that makes the audience feel seen and accompanied. The Caregiver ships with warmth and regularity. They show up whether or not the campaign is live.

The **Creator** ships the work. The thing they made. The process of making it. The standard they held. The Creator ships with craft and ships when the work earns it.

The **Ruler** ships the standard. The declaration of what excellence looks like. The Ruler ships less frequently and with full confidence. Quality over quantity. Authority over volume.

The **Everyperson** ships the truth. The plain-spoken observation. The thing everyone was thinking and nobody was saying. The Everyperson ships conversationally, like a text from a smart friend, regularly and without fuss.

The **Sage** ships the insight. The piece of content that gives the audience something genuinely useful they could not have gotten anywhere else. The Sage ships when the insight is real. Never to fill a content calendar.

The **Innocent** ships the proof of the promise. The demonstration that the thing they said is true. The ingredient. The process. The person behind it. The Innocent ships with simplicity and ships to confirm, not to impress.

One Dare

Before you go to Chapter 14, do one thing.

Ship something.

Not the brand playbook. Not the website launch. Not the full campaign. One thing. A LinkedIn post. An email to your list. A rewrite of your homepage headline. A piece of content written from your archetype's voice using one of the 12 frameworks.

One thing. Today.

Not because it will be perfect. Because the compounding starts when you ship the first thing, not when you finish planning the system.

You know who you are. You know your story. You know your voice. You know your audience.

Now go be in front of them.

Brand Deck Connection: Summary Card 5, Activation Prompts.

The overview of all eight Activation Prompts in Chapter 14. Each one is a creative dare designed to produce something real: a piece of content, a campaign brief, a team exercise, a proof of concept. Pull the card before you read the chapter. The dare on the front is the brief. The back is the how.

Next: Chapter 14. The 8 Activation Prompts.

Creative fuel. Real output. No excuses.

CHAPTER 14:
The 8 Activation Prompts

"An idea that is not dangerous is unworthy of being called an idea at all."

-- Oscar Wilde

Eight prompts.

Each one is a dare. Not a framework to study. A provocation designed to produce something real: a piece of content, a campaign brief, a team exercise, a conversation that has been waiting to happen.

None of them are comfortable. That is not an accident. The most useful thing a prompt can do is make you slightly uncomfortable and then make it impossible to stop thinking about the question it raised.

For each prompt you get the dare, the brief, which archetypes feel it most naturally, a brand example of it working in the wild, and the output: what you should have in your hands when you are done.

Work through the ones that feel most alive. Come back to the ones that made you uncomfortable. Those are usually the most important.

PROMPT 1: The Unfair Comparison

"Compare yourself to something you have no business being compared to."

The Dare

Find the unexpected analogy. The thing from an entirely different world that illuminates exactly what your brand is and why it matters. Not a competitor comparison. Not a category benchmark. Something that comes from left field and lands like truth.

Old Spice is not a deodorant. It is a ridiculous action movie you watch every morning before work.

Notion is not project management software. It is the blank page that doesn't judge you for how you organize your thoughts.

Peloton is not a bike. It is the coach who shows up even when you don't feel like it.

The Brief

Complete this sentence: "[Your brand] is not [the obvious category descriptor]. It is [the unexpected, true, slightly surprising thing it actually is for the people who love it most]."

Write five versions. Throw out the first three. The fourth is usually interesting. The fifth is usually right.

Then build a piece of content around the fifth one. A LinkedIn post. A campaign brief. An About page rewrite. One thing, built on the unexpected true comparison.

Best Archetype Pairs

Jester, Magician, Rebel, Creator.

The Jester finds the absurd version and makes it funny and true at the same time. The Magician finds the transformative frame that makes the ordinary extraordinary. The Rebel finds the version that rejects the category entirely. The Creator finds the version that is about making something.

In the Wild

Liquid Death spent years refusing to be compared to other water brands. They compared themselves to heavy metal. A water company compared to heavy metal. The comparison is absurd. It is also exactly right for everything the brand is, and it attracted an audience that water brands had never reached before because water brands had never tried to speak to them.

Output

One piece of published content built on your unfair comparison. Not a draft. Published. Today counts. Tomorrow counts. This week absolutely counts. Next quarter does not.

PROMPT 2: The Enemy Manifesto

"Name the thing you're fighting. Out loud. In public."

The Dare

Write your brand's Enemy Manifesto. Not a competitor attack. The thing you are fundamentally against. The condition, the attitude, the status quo that your brand exists to disrupt, displace, or destroy.

Patagonia's enemy is the way the world produces and discards. Not a competitor. A condition.

Mailchimp's enemy was the complexity that kept small businesses from doing email marketing. Not Constant Contact. Gatekeeping.

Popcorn GTM's enemy is the restaurant tech brand that sounds exactly like every other restaurant tech brand and wonders why nobody remembers them. Not an agency. A failure mode.

The Brief

Write five sentences. Each one names something your brand is against and why it is against it. The enemy should be a real thing that your natural audience is also against. The manifesto is not a rant. It is a declaration of shared values expressed as shared refusals.

Start each sentence with: "We are done with..."

Best Archetype Pairs

Rebel, Hero, Ruler, Creator.

The Rebel's enemy manifesto is a declaration of war. The Hero's is a rallying cry. The Ruler's is a statement of standards that the enemy violates. The Creator's is a refusal to compromise craft.

In the Wild

BrewDog's early Equity for Punks manifesto named its enemies with gleeful specificity. Corporate beer. The homogenization of taste. The distribution system that kept craft beer out of reach. Every enemy named was something their natural audience was also sick of. The manifesto became a founding document for a community because the community shared the enemies.

Output

A five-sentence Enemy Manifesto. Publishable. Post it on LinkedIn. Put it on your About page. Read it at the start of your next team meeting. The reaction will tell you everything about whether the people around you share your brand's worldview or whether you have more alignment work to do.

PROMPT 3: The Thing You've Never Said Out Loud

"What does your brand actually think? Not the PR answer. The real one."

The Dare

Every brand has things it thinks but hasn't said publicly because it seemed risky, controversial, or just too honest.

Those things are almost always more valuable than the safe version of the brand's opinion.

What does your brand actually think about the category it's in? What does it think about the way most brands in the space operate? What does it think about the future of the industry? About the conventional wisdom everyone accepts that is probably wrong?

Name it. Clearly. Publicly.

The Brief

Write the piece of thought leadership that your brand has been avoiding. Not aggressive. Not a competitor attack. Just honest. The thing that, if you said it in a room of industry peers, would make some people nod vigorously and other people look slightly uncomfortable.

The nods are your natural audience confirming their worldview. The discomfort is everyone else. Both responses tell you the content is real.

Best Archetype Pairs

Sage, Rebel, Explorer, Hero.

The Sage's unsaid thing is usually a hard truth wrapped in data. The Rebel's is a declaration that the emperor has no clothes. The Explorer's is a finding from somewhere the category hasn't been yet. The Hero's is a challenge to an industry that has gotten complacent.

In the Wild

When David Ogilvy said "the consumer isn't a moron, she's your wife," it was the thing the advertising industry had never said publicly about itself: that most advertising condescended to the audience it claimed to serve. The industry heard it. Half of it was angry. Half of it was relieved. The ones who were relieved found their people.

Output

One published piece of thought leadership built on your brand's real opinion. Medium length: 300-500 words. Pick a platform where your natural audience lives and post it there. Respond to every comment, including the pushback. The conversation it starts is the point.

PROMPT 4: The 24-Hour Brand Experiment

"Try the thing you've been theorizing about."

The Dare

Pick one element of your brand voice, story, or audience positioning that you have been thinking about but haven't tested. The new archetype-driven headline. The Enemy Manifesto tone. The vulnerability of the Origin Story. The boldness of the Rebel's Contrast Manifesto.

Give it 24 hours in the real world.

Not a full campaign. Not a full website rewrite. One post. One email. One piece of content. Minimum viable. Specific. On-voice.

The Brief

Choose the thing you've been holding back. Not the entire rebrand. The one element. The sentence you wrote and then deleted because it seemed too direct, too honest, too specific, too committed.

Put it in a piece of content today. Publish it. Observe.

Does it attract the right response? Not necessarily agreement. Resonance. The feeling from your natural audience that you said something worth saying?

Best Archetype Pairs

All of them. Every archetype has something it's been holding back. The Innocent has been too afraid to admit the harder parts of holding its standards. The Sage has an insight it hasn't shared because it contradicts the consensus. The Jester has a bit it hasn't deployed because it seemed too risky. The Caregiver has a story about a customer moment it hasn't told because it seemed too small.

None of these things are too small. None of them are too risky for a 24-hour experiment.

In the Wild

Most of the great brand voice moments that became defining, the Old Spice shower reply campaign, Wendy's Twitter voice, Dollar Shave Club's launch video, started as experiments. Someone decided to try the thing instead of keep planning it. The response told them it was right. The brand evolved from there.

Output

One piece of content, published in 24 hours, built on the element you've been holding. Document the response. What did it produce? What does that tell you about your audience? What does it tell you about your archetype? Use the data. Run the next experiment.

PROMPT 5: The Rewrite Everything

"What would this look like if we actually sounded like us?"

The Dare

Take the single most important piece of public-facing copy your brand has. The homepage headline. The LinkedIn bio. The elevator pitch. The first email in your welcome sequence.

Rewrite it completely through your primary archetype's voice using one of the 12 frameworks.

Not a light edit. A complete rewrite. Start from zero. The only brief is your archetype and one framework.

The Brief

Step one: pull the current copy.

Step two: run the Voice Rinse Test (Chapter 8, Tool 6). Remove the brand name. Ask if anyone would know it's you.

Step three: rewrite it. Full archetype. Full framework. No compromise with the old version.

Step four: show both versions to five people who know your brand. Ask: which one sounds more like us?

Step five: publish the winner.

Best Archetype Pairs

All archetypes. Every brand has copy that was written before the archetype was clear or that was written by committee and lost the voice somewhere in revision. The Rewrite Everything exercise finds that copy and fixes it.

In the Wild

When Slack rewrote their homepage from "A messaging app for teams" to content that communicated the actual experience of using it, the conversion rate improved significantly. The rewrite was not adding more features. It was finding the voice that had been present in the product but absent in the marketing.

Output

One rewritten piece of critical copy, published. The old version archived for comparison. A note on what changed and why. This note is valuable content in itself: the story of the brand finding its voice is exactly the kind of origin content your natural audience wants to read.

PROMPT 6: The Collaboration Dare

"Who else lives in your archetype's world?"

The Dare

Find a creator, brand, or individual who shares your archetype's worldview, your audience's belonging signals, and your brand's conviction. Not a competitor. A fellow traveler.

Build something together.

A podcast episode. A co-authored piece of content. A joint activation. A shared event. A conversation published in public.

The Brief

The collaboration should feel like two people from the same world discovering they have been thinking about the same thing.

The Sage partners with another Sage to work through a difficult question in public. The Rebel partners with a photographer, a musician, a filmmaker who shares the refusal. The Explorer teams up with someone who has been somewhere similar and is reporting back from a different angle. The Creator collaborates with someone whose craft illuminates something about your own.

The test: does the collaboration make both parties more interesting? Does it put both brands in front of the right audience?

Best Archetype Pairs

Explorer, Creator, Sage, Lover.

These archetypes have the most to gain from collaboration because their audience values curation and taste. Being seen with the right partners sends a signal that no ad campaign can send.

In the Wild

Patagonia's editorial collaborations with environmental journalists and scientists are not advertising. They are the brand finding its fellow travelers and building something with them. The audience for those collaborations is exactly the audience Patagonia wants to deepen its relationship with.

Output

One collaboration, scoped and initiated. Not completed. Initiated. Send the email. Make the ask. Define the brief. The output from this prompt is the conversation that starts the collaboration, not the collaboration itself. The conversation is the dare.

PROMPT 7: The Customer Story Sprint

"Let someone else make your case."

The Dare

Find your best customer story. The one where the transformation was most specific, most human, most clearly before-and-after. The one where the customer used language that made you think "that is better than anything we've ever written about ourselves."

Turn it into a piece of content that is primarily about them.

Not a case study formatted like a business document. A story. The hero's journey of a specific person who found your brand at a specific moment and experienced a specific transformation.

The Brief

Call or email the customer. Ask them to tell you the story. Record it. The best quotes are in the telling, not in the written version they would give you if you asked for a testimonial.

Listen for: the before state (specific and uncomfortable), the moment of decision (what finally made them move), the transformation (what changed and how they know), and the after state (what their world looks like now).

Build the story from those four elements. Use their language wherever possible. Your brand is a supporting character. The customer is the hero.

Best Archetype Pairs

Caregiver, Hero, Creator, Everyperson.

The Caregiver's customer story is about the moment they felt genuinely accompanied. The Hero's is about the transformation achieved through effort. The Creator's is about the thing the customer made possible with your tools. The Everyperson's is about the relief of something that finally just worked.

In the Wild

Airbnb's "Belong Anywhere" stories are almost entirely customer stories. The brand is nearly invisible. The person, the place, the specific experience: those are the content. The brand earns credit by making the experience possible. That restraint is what makes the content extraordinary.

Output

One customer story, written and published. 300-500 words. Named or anonymized depending on the customer's preference. With a quote in their language that you did not sanitize because it was too specific or too human. That specificity is the point.

PROMPT 8: The Brand Playbook Preview

"Show your work."

The Dare

Share a piece of your brand thinking publicly.

Not the finished playbook. Not the polished brand guide. A piece of the thinking in progress. The archetype you chose and why. The voice recipe and what it produced. The audience insight that changed how you write. The framework you are using to tell your story.

Show the work.

The Brief

The most trusted brands are the ones that show how they think. Transparency about process is more credible than confidence about results. The audience that watches a brand figure something out develops a loyalty that no amount of polished positioning can produce.

Pick one element of your brand thinking. The archetype decision. The voice choice. The audience insight. The Enemy Manifesto. Write a 300-word post about how you got there and what changed when you did.

Be specific. Be honest. Include the part where you weren't sure.

Best Archetype Pairs

Sage, Creator, Explorer, Everyperson.

The Sage shows their thinking as a form of teaching. The Creator shows their process as proof of craft. The Explorer shares the finding from the journey. The Everyperson shares honestly because that is what peers do.

In the Wild

Basecamp published their entire business philosophy, their brand voice, their product decisions, all of it publicly, in the form of books, blog posts, and public arguments. The audience they built is the most loyal in their category precisely because they know how Basecamp thinks. The transparency is the brand.

Output

One published piece of transparent brand thinking. The working document, not the finished document. What you decided. Why you decided it. What changed as a result. Your natural audience will find this more compelling than a finished brand video. And the people who find it will be exactly the ones you are building this brand for.

Prompt Rotation

You do not do all eight at once.

You pick the one that is most alive right now, the one that produced the most internal resistance when you read it (resistance is signal), or the one that solves the most urgent problem your brand is facing.

Do that one. Fully. Produce the output.

Then wait. Look at what the output produced in terms of audience response, internal clarity, momentum.

Then pick the next one.

The eight prompts are a permanent creative resource. Come back to them quarterly. The one that seemed irrelevant six months ago may be exactly right today. The one you deployed successfully can be run again with a different frame.

This is the activation system. It does not expire. It compounds.

Brand Deck Connection: Activation Prompt Cards 1-8.

Each prompt in this chapter has a corresponding Brand Deck card with the dare on the front and the full brief and output guidance on the back. Pull the deck before a team creative session. Fan out all eight cards. Ask the room: which one are we most afraid of? Start there.

Next: Chapter 15. Build Your Brand Playbook.

Take everything in this book and turn it into the working document your whole team can actually use.

CHAPTER 15:
Build Your Brand Playbook

"A system is just a way of doing something that works consistently. Build the system. Then forget you built it and just do the thing."

You have done the work.

You have an archetype. You have a story. You have a voice. You know your audience. You have the frameworks, the tools, the prompts.

What you do not yet have is the document that makes all of that work available to everyone in your organization, in every context, on every day that is not this one.

That is the **Brand Playbook.**

Not a brand bible. Not a 60-page PDF that lives in Google Drive until the designer needs to find the logo. A working document. Short enough to read. Specific enough to act on. Built to be used, not admired.

This chapter gives you the template and the instructions for building it.

What the Brand Playbook Is Not

Before you build the thing, know what you are not building.

It is not a style guide.

A style guide tells you what font to use and how many pixels of padding go around the logo. That document has its place. This is not that document. The Playbook lives at a level above production specifications.

It is not a brand deck.

A brand deck tells the story of the brand to an external audience: investors, press, partners. The Playbook is internal. It tells the story of the brand to the people building it.

It is not a strategy document.

Strategy documents explain why decisions were made and what the plan is. The Playbook is the distillation of those decisions into actionable standards. It does not argue. It declares.

It is not a one-time deliverable.

The biggest mistake brands make with their Playbook is treating it as a project with a completion date. The Playbook is a living document. It gets updated as the brand evolves, as the voice sharpens, as the audience understanding deepens. The date on the last revision is a health signal. If it hasn't been touched in a year, something is wrong.

The One-Page Brand Brief

The core of the Playbook. Everything else supports this.

One page. Every essential element. Specific enough to write from, design from, hire from, and brief an agency or AI tool from.

Here is the complete structure:

BRAND BRIEF: [BRAND NAME]

Last updated: [date]

WHO WE ARE

Primary Archetype: [Name] — [One-sentence description of the archetype in your brand's specific context]

Secondary Archetype: [Name] — [How it serves the primary]

Core Belief: [The single conviction that defines everything your brand does. One sentence. The thing you would hold even if it cost you a customer.]

Our Origin in one sentence: [Why this brand needed to exist. Not the company history. The human reason.]

WHO WE'RE FOR

Natural Audience: [Psychographic portrait. Not demographics. What they believe. What they fear. Where they are going.]

The story we share: [The single sentence where your brand's worldview and your audience's worldview are the same thing.]

What we make possible: [The transformation. The before and after in plain language.]

HOW WE SOUND

Voice Recipe:

- [Attribute 1]: [percentage]%
- [Attribute 2]: [percentage]%
- [Attribute 3]: [percentage]%
- [Attribute 4 if applicable]: [percentage]%

Sounds Like: [2-3 sentences that exemplify the voice at its best]

Does Not Sound Like: [2-3 sentences that exemplify the voice at its worst / most off-brand]

WHAT WE NEVER DO

9. [Specific prohibition. One sentence.]
10. [Specific prohibition. One sentence.]
11. [Specific prohibition. One sentence.]

OUR PRIMARY STORYTELLING FRAMEWORK

[Framework name] — [One sentence on why this framework fits this archetype and this brand's primary story]

That is the Brief. Every element, one page, nothing omitted.

If you can hand this page to a writer you have never worked with and get back something that sounds like your brand, the Brief is working.

If you get back something that sounds generic, the Brief is not specific enough. Go back to the relevant chapter and sharpen the element that failed.

The Supporting Sections

The One-Page Brief is the core. These supporting sections make the
Playbook complete.

Section 1: Voice Samples

A minimum of five examples of your brand's voice done right. Real
published content from your brand that passes the Voice Rinse Test. These
are the reference examples. When someone asks "what does on-brand
sound like?" the answer is these five pieces, not an adjective list.

Update this section every six months. Retire old examples that no longer
represent your current voice. Add new ones as you produce your best work.

Section 2: The Nope List

The complete version of Tool 5 from Chapter 8. Every specific word, phrase,
construction, and tone that is definitionally off-brand. Organized by
category. Updated when new category clichés emerge that need to be added
to the prohibited list.

This section does more to prevent voice drift than any style guide ever
written.

Section 3: The Archetype Card

A one-page summary of your primary archetype. The character profile, the
four defining traits, the voice in action (sounds like / does not sound like),
and the key Red Flags specific to your archetype that you monitor for.

This is the context that makes everything else make sense. Someone new to
the brand who reads the Brief and then reads the Archetype Card should be
able to produce on-brand content within a week.

Section 4: The Audience Portrait

A two-page synthesis of the eight Audience Insight cards you built in
Chapter 11. The belief inventory, the fear map at all three levels, the
aspiration portrait, and the decision trigger profile, assembled into a
cohesive picture of the human being you are building this brand for.

This section answers the question "who are we writing for?" whenever anyone at the company has to make a content decision.

Section 5: The Brand Deck Integration

A reference to which Brand Deck cards are most active in your current brand work. Which archetype card, which storytelling frameworks you are running, which voice tools are in regular use, which audience insight tools you return to most often. This connects the Playbook to the physical card system so they function as one tool, not two separate things.

How to Brief Anyone with the Playbook

The Playbook's job is to be handable. To anyone. With enough context that they produce something good.

Here is how to use it for three specific scenarios.

Briefing a new team member:

Hand them the Playbook on day one. Walk them through the One-Page Brief. Show them the five voice samples. Ask them to write one piece of content before their first week is out, any format, any length, just using the voice they just read. Give feedback specifically: this part is on-voice, this part isn't, here is the specific adjustment.

The feedback makes the Playbook real. The Playbook makes the feedback make sense. Both together build the shared understanding faster than any onboarding document.

Briefing an agency or freelancer:

Send the Playbook as the creative brief. Not a brief about the specific project. The Playbook itself, plus a one-paragraph description of the specific deliverable and its audience.

The agency that reads the Playbook and still produces something generic either did not read it or is not the right agency. The Playbook is a filter. The response to it tells you whether you have the right partner.

Briefing an AI tool:

The Playbook is the system prompt. Paste the One-Page Brief, the five voice samples, and the Nope List as context before any content generation request. The output quality difference is significant and immediate. The AI is not guessing at your brand's voice. It has the recipe.

Update the system prompt when the Playbook updates. The AI brief goes stale the same way any creative brief goes stale.

Keeping the Playbook Alive

A Playbook that isn't updated isn't a Playbook. It's an artifact.

Here is the minimum maintenance schedule:

Monthly: Review the Nope List. Has new industry jargon emerged that needs to be added? Has the category started using a phrase that used to feel fine and now feels like everyone's using it? Add it.

Quarterly: Run the Voice Rinse Test on five recent pieces of content. Do they pass? If not, what is drifting? Address the specific element that is off and note it in the Playbook.

Biannually: Update the Voice Samples. Replace anything older than eighteen months or anything that no longer represents your best work. Add the two or three pieces from the past six months that best exemplify the voice.

Annually: Full Playbook review. Has the archetype evolved? Has the audience picture shifted? Has the core belief been refined by a year of experience? This is the one time per year to revisit the foundation and confirm it still reflects who the brand actually is.

If the brand has changed significantly, the Playbook should reflect that change. A Playbook that no longer matches the brand is not a Playbook. It is a history document.

The Brand Deck as an Ongoing Tool

The Playbook is the document. The Brand Deck is the living system.

The cards are designed to be picked up, worked through, and returned to. Not as a one-time exercise but as a regular practice. A quarterly workshop. A team creative session. A solo exercise when you are stuck.

Here is a practical ongoing ritual:

At the start of any significant content project, pull three Brand Deck cards. Your archetype card. The framework card for the structure you're using. One audience insight card for the audience you're speaking to.

Read them before you write. They recalibrate. They remind you who you are, how you tell your story, and who you're telling it to. The three cards take five minutes to review. The content that follows from that review is better than the content that follows from opening a blank document and hoping.

The Brand Deck is not a tool you master. It is a tool you return to. The returning is the practice. The practice is the discipline. The discipline is what makes the brand consistent across time, team, and channel.

The Thing Nobody Tells You About Brand Work

Building a brand is not a project. It is a practice.

There is no moment of completion. There is no point at which the brand is finished and you can stop paying attention to it. The brand is alive as long as the organization is alive. It evolves. It grows. It occasionally needs recalibration.

The brands that endure are not the ones with the most perfect positioning documents. They are the ones with the people inside them who remain intentional about who the brand is and consistent about expressing it.

The Playbook makes that intention portable. Specific. Teachable. The discipline of returning to it is what keeps the intention alive when the day-to-day pressure of running a business pushes it to the periphery.

Keep the Playbook alive. Keep the cards in the room. Keep asking the questions that got you here:

Who are we, at the bone?

What story do only we tell?

Who are we for?

What do we make possible for them?

Those questions do not expire. The answers get sharper every time you ask them.

You Are Ready

This is where the book ends and the work begins.

Not begins again. The work in this book was already the work. Every archetype exercise, every story framework you considered, every voice tool you ran, every audience insight you uncovered: that was the work. Real work that produced real clarity.

The Playbook is how that clarity survives Monday morning.

Build it. Use it. Update it. Hand it to the next person who joins your team and watch them build something on-brand in a week instead of a quarter.

Then go back to Chapter 13 and ship something.

The compounding starts now.

Next: The Conclusion (aka The End.)

Your brand, claimed.

The AMA definition revisited. And the pen passed to you.

THIS IS THE END, MY ONLY FRIEND, THE END:
Your Brand, Claimed

We started with a definition.

"The activity, set of institutions, and processes for creating, communicating, delivering, and exchanging offerings that have value for customers, clients, partners, and society at large."

Twenty-six words. The American Marketing Association's official definition of marketing. Written by a committee. Approved by consensus. Used by professors, practitioners, and certification programs around the world.

It includes the words "creating," "communicating," "delivering," "exchanging," and "value."

It does not include the words "meaning," "identity," or "story."

You are not the same reader you were when you read that sentence the first time.

You know now what the absence means. The definition is technically complete. It describes what marketing does at the mechanical level. The plumbing. It does not describe what makes the plumbing worth anything. It does not describe what flows through it.

That absence is not an oversight. That absence is an entire field of knowledge that the textbook decided was too slippery to include, too human to systematize, too archetypal to put in a framework.

This book has been about that absence.

Here is what you now know.

The brands that endure, the ones that earn loyalty and command premium and survive disruption and become part of how their customers describe themselves, do not endure because they executed the five-step process correctly.

They endure because they knew who they were.

They had an archetype. A character. A way of seeing the world and a way of expressing that view that was specific enough to attract the right people and honest enough to keep them.

They had a story. Not a value proposition or a messaging matrix. A story. The kind that sticks because it is structured and true and aimed at a specific human being's deepest need to see themselves reflected in something larger than a product.

They had a voice. Not adjectives on a wall. Choices made consistently over time until the pattern became unmistakable. A fingerprint. The kind of presence that survives the logo being removed.

They knew their audience. Not a demographic profile. A human portrait. What they believed, what they feared, where they were going, and what finally made them move.

They activated. They shipped. They built the compounding advantage that only comes from being in front of your audience while your competitors are still deciding.

You have all of this now.

The market does not decide who your brand is.

You do.

The market responds to who you are. The right people find you, or they don't. The wrong people self-select out, or they don't. The difference is how clearly and consistently you express the identity you have now claimed.

Claimed is the right word. An archetype is not assigned. It is not discovered in a workshop and then filed away. It is claimed. Actively. Repeatedly. In every piece of content, every product decision, every hire, every customer interaction, every policy, every response to a crisis.

You claim it by expressing it.

You lose it by not.

The AMA definition is still 26 words. It still doesn't include meaning, identity, or story.

That gap is not going to close. The institutions that build those definitions are not reading this book. They are teaching the next generation of marketers to understand the marketplace and customers, to develop customer-driven marketing strategy, to construct integrated programs that deliver value.

Those marketers will be competent.

The ones who also read this book will be dangerous.

Go claim your brand.

You know who you are.

"The myth is the public dream. The dream is the private myth."

-- Joseph Campbell

The story was always yours. You just needed to know its shape.